I Am Who God Says I Am

I Am Who God Says I Am

Taking on the Family Name

SHAVONNE R. RUFFIN

RESOURCE *Publications* • Eugene, Oregon

I AM WHO GOD SAYS I AM
Taking on the Family Name

Copyright © 2022 Shavonne R. Ruffin. All rights reserved. Except for brief quotations in critical publications or reviews, no part of this book may be reproduced in any manner without prior written permission from the publisher. Write: Permissions, Wipf and Stock Publishers, 199 W. 8th Ave., Suite 3, Eugene, OR 97401.

Resource Publications
An Imprint of Wipf and Stock Publishers
199 W. 8th Ave., Suite 3
Eugene, OR 97401

www.wipfandstock.com

PAPERBACK ISBN: 978-1-6667-5846-7
HARDCOVER ISBN: 978-1-6667-5847-4
EBOOK ISBN: 978-1-6667-5848-1

VERSION NUMBER 101322

To my parents, Senora and Cornell,
thank you for teaching me who I am.

God is, therefore I am.

Contents

Abbreviations | viii

Introduction | 1

Chapter 1
I am a Child of God. | 13

Chapter 2
I am God's treasure. | 27

Chapter 3
I am the righteousness of God. | 40

Chapter 4
I am the temple of God. | 49

Chapter 5
I am God's workmanship. | 58

Chapter 6
I am fearfully and wonderfully made. | 68

Chapter 7
I am the salt of the Earth. | 79

Chapter 8
I am the light of God. | 88

Chapter 9
I am an overcomer. | 99

Chapter 10
I am predestined. | 115

Bibliography | 129

Abbreviations

AMB—Amplified Bible
ESV—English Standard Version
ISV—International Standard Version
KJV—King James Version
NIV—New International Version
NLT—New Living Translation

Introduction

FASHIONISTA, STYLE GURU, MISTRESS of Cloth. Any of those names would've sufficed to describe me in high school. Most of my peers dressed for rural country life: sneakers and blue jeans. I guess you could call it country chic. I'm sure Dorothy and the Scarecrow would have been proud. However, I wouldn't be caught dead in those clothes or following a yellow brick road, for that matter. I was different, so I dressed differently. My friends liked stomping in their Air Force Ones, while I preferred to strut in sky-high heels with the shortest mini skirt that defied the school's dress code. I walked the school's halls like my personal catwalk, my own modest runway.

I loved fashion and loved shopping for it even more. So when I stumbled upon the most beautiful fascinator, I knew I had to have it. It was stunning and could have been worn at any royal family affair or at least been on the set of Clueless. I spent my entire savings on the magnificent array of black and silver flowers, ensuring I resembled my fashion icons, Dionne and Cher. So, I went to school wearing my fashion-forward headband, which did its purpose as my peers and teachers were indeed fascinated.

Then it happened. A few girls from the opposing table began to murmur as I sat eating my lunch. The murmurs went from snickering, and snickering went from full-blown laughter. They were amused, more like falling out laughing at me and my new head attire. I honestly felt like Cher when she was rejected by Christian, totally bummed. Those girls were fashion victims, and

I was a fashion icon. Unfortunately, that group didn't think so at that moment. They laughed, continuously pointing to my head like monstrous weeds were sprouting instead of magnificent flowers.

I vividly remember the teasing and bullying that lasted the entire length of lunch. Methodically moving my peas from one side to the next, I blinked away the tears. I wouldn't cry; I wouldn't give those girls the satisfaction of seeing one tear fall on my cheek. Instead, I decided never to wear that stupid headband again.

Oddly, I never understood the purpose of that moment until now. There are two things that God is revealing to me. First, we allow a few to rob us of our identity as our individuality has worth. Our identities are tied to our anointing, which comes with the highest costs. Even though my headpiece was worth no more than a fast-food restaurant combo, it took time to acquire it.

Our anointing is a part of our identity, which often comes from suffering: the death of a child, a loved one, homelessness, disease, or sickness. However, we tend to discount what makes us into what God has called us to be. We have a propensity to throw our anointings cost away like it was as meaningless as a fashion accessory.

The second thing God is revealing is that our identities are not only valuable but are spiritually manufactured. The fact is that God purchased us before we were even worth acquiring. We all have free will to choose him or not. However, the bottom line is that God purchased us before we were spiritually made. Not too many people can afford to buy something without seeing it first. Even if it is custom-made, we simply give a down payment until the final product is produced. God did not provide a downpayment but paid for us in full with the Blood of Jesus Christ. We are not finished being made, but he died for the finished product he sees in us.

We ultimately say that the Blood was not enough when we discount our worth. Believers cannot be so cavalier with what God purchased and produced internally within his Creation. God is our Creator, designer, manufacturer, and inventor. Unfortunately, we allow others to invade what God has made. Our identities were

INTRODUCTION

created by an almighty God who equipped us with every personality and talent that makes us uniquely prepared in him.

All day long, I wore my headband. However, I quickly removed it after a few uncomfortable minutes. I developed my fashion persona for years, only to demolish my fashion identity within a half-hour. Fashion was who I was. I knew color coordination and even understood the fifty shades of gray before that phrase became a title that made housewives blush. However, it didn't matter. Nothing mattered if girls who thought wearing baggy t-shirts and jeans thought I looked ridiculous.

Maybe I did. That entire day, I received compliments upon compliments concerning my headband. Yet, every compliment received could not undo the teasing. My identity had been mocked, so I did the most logical thing a fourteen-year-old girl could do. I threw it away.

My beautiful silver and black crown found its new home in a Hefty garbage bag. It could accessorize the rubbish as I refused to be victimized because of a stupid accessory. The headband was not the only thing that I threw away. Sure, my fascinator had value, but so did my identity, and both took a significant hit.

I loved that fascinator, but most importantly, I loved the person I was. Most teenagers undergo identity crises during adolescence. They try to figure out where they fit in; who they want to be. However, I never had those problems. I knew I liked being different, dressing peculiarly, and having my own distinct style. I marched to the beat of my own drum. Apparently, I only marched when everyone else didn't mind my beat.

Nevertheless, those girls did mind. They didn't care about my symbolic rhythmic tapping. Nor did they care about my positive strides as I typically walked through life carefree. Unfortunately, I didn't think I cared what others thought as long as they liked who I was.

Boy, was I wrong; I did care. Everyone that day marveled at my headpiece, and all I could do was focus on those unruly girls who seemed to want to tear me from stem to sternum. I could have possibly taken a few snickers, a few laughs. However, those girls were literally threatening to snatch my headband directly off my head. I was terrified because my fascinator was connected to my hair, my hair to my head, and my head to the rest of my body. If they got the headband, my entire body would be in jeopardy.

I couldn't let that happen. It was an obvious choice, toss the headpiece or off with my head. Since I had my head longer, I decided the headband had to go. I knew my friends and teachers would question what happened to my fascinator, but the small group of girls looked more considerable than the masses, and I valued not being beaten to a bloody pulp.

I doubt my headband would have produced World War III. However, those girls were quite intimidating. They were larger, a little rough around the edges, and seemed to have bowling balls for breast compared to my modest oranges. Even though I was popular and had friends who would not have allowed my life to end during lunch, I still felt like those girls filled the entire cafeteria. They were only about three or four of them, but it seemed like the whole room, including the lunch ladies, was against me.

Isn't it funny that when faced with opposers concerning our identities, Satan will multiply our eyesight to see hundreds of people against us when it is only a mere few? I had the entire cafeteria on my side, yet I only saw four girls. Surely, I could have stood up to them. I could have told them why I liked my headband. I could have even shown them fashion magazines where teen models wore similar headpieces. Nonetheless, I didn't. The small group seemed to outnumber the hundreds. Therefore, I sat closed-mouthed, not having enough courage to defend my headband or identity.

Incredibly, we allow a small, insignificant number to cheat us out of our God-given uniqueness. God creates each of his children, molding us into what he needs us to be. He designs us perfectly, giving us our personalities, strengths, and weaknesses. Then, when faced with obstacles, we forget our Creator but focus on a few who attempt to discredit the workmanship of God. Even if the entire world is against us, we only need three, the Father, the Son, and the Holy Ghost. However, we focus solely on people who don't matter when God has the final say over our lives. He has designed our course, yet we become afraid of the small group without considering an enormous God.

Unfortunately, fourteen-year-old me was unconcerned about my God-given identity but concerned myself with worry, which manifested into full-blown anxiety and panic attacks. Sleeplessly, I tossed and turned that night, worrying about those girls. The headband remained in the garbage, but I was still concerned. That group looked like huge giants with monstrous teeth, and I was about three apples high. They were freakishly large for teenagers, and every time I thought about them, I made myself sick with worry until I prayed. That night I prayed on a snot-covered pillow that I would not worry about that situation or any other one for that matter.

Thankfully, God answered my prayer. I went to school and wasn't bothered by the bloodcurdling bullying. Mercifully, those girls had moved on to their next victim. Relieved, I decided I wouldn't do anything to ruffle their feathers. I would put my symbolic drum back in its case. I would sit quietly during lunch. I would even start attempting to buy into the chic country look. However, most importantly, I would never wear that fascinator again. In other words, I wouldn't be myself.

As believers, we are too quick to deny who we are based on others' thoughts and opinions about us in the natural and the spiritual. A person who appreciates their individuality does not hinder someone else's. Instead, they encourage them while perfecting their own. Fourteen-year-old me was a vibrant young lady full of life and loved being different. Subsequently, I hid that part of myself throughout my 8th-grade year because of that one incident.

Ironically, three years later, I saw those same girls wearing fascinators. Unfortunately, they were outdated and out of style. I then recognized that sometimes people tease you because they want to be who you are. Gratefully, I emerged back into that unique girl as I realized that I could not be cheated out of my identity. Nevertheless, this does not mean that I was never in denial of who I was.

In 2019, my grandmother died, and not only did I lose her, but I lost my identity again. For decades, I delighted in being the granddaughter of our esteemed presiding bishop. Growing up, she was the definition of Christian royalty. When anyone questioned my family lineage, I would smile, gracefully nod, and recall I was her granddaughter. That seemed enough, as all knew her to be a remarkable lady, and most importantly, I was her eldest granddaughter. I would marvel at her respect, believing that respect trickled down to me as well. I would never take advantage of her being the bishop of several churches, yet I knew that my identity was wrapped into me being her beloved. She was the queen, and I was the queen's granddaughter.

Not even twenty-four hours had passed after her death, and the church stated that we must move forward. Everything seemed to move quickly while I was stagnated by grief. I just stared at the empty seat where she would no longer sit, the queen's chair. In her place was a black cloth instead, signifying her death. The vice-bishop, or now the new presiding prelate, came to our church to encourage the congregation that we must keep moving, that we could not allow our adversary to take advantage of this moment. At that second, I realized that I was no longer the bishop's granddaughter, and a shift in the royal family had occurred.

I had lost my identity. No one besides my daughter lost more that day than me. I had lost my presiding prelate, pastor, grandmother, friend, and who I was. A few weeks later, one of my aunts told me my grandmother had to die so I could be elevated. I knew what she meant, for God had revealed that my grandmother was a crutch for me. Even though my grandmother had the highest authority in our church organization, my family knew she would stifle my leadership. Not intentionally, but because she was worried about what others in the church may think. It appeared that through her death, a new identity would be found.

Many people thought I would be her incarnate now, for the most part. Like somehow, her inner spirit would descend like a dove to make me the new her. Even on her deathbed, I told my grandmother I was strong and would ensure that the church

INTRODUCTION

would continue. I never lied to my grandmother until then. The ugly truth is that I was not as strong in God as I thought. There was no way I could fulfill fifty-five years of ministry like she did. I only had my initial sermon five months ago, and my biggest supporter was now leaving me. Nope, I was not the new her and was not too accepting of this latest self. Therefore, I did what I did best, sabotage.

Spiritual sabotage was my gateway to committing slow spiritual suicide. I stopped fasting, praying, and reading God's Word. For months, I had even stopped going to church. If she died naturally, then I'd die spiritually. I was slowly killing my spiritual man, choking the life out of him. There was no one any longer that held me accountable, like my grandmother, except for my inner man. Therefore, he must die. Yes, a new identity was emerging, and it was not good.

Social distancing became my murderous accomplice as it gave me an excuse for a slow spiritual death. Once we were permitted church services in the parking lot, I could comfortably sit in my car, attending but not in attendance. I put on a good front, half-listening to the pastor while watching the clock, ready to leave. I didn't want to be there as I would peer over at my grandmother's house many days, watching to see if she would come outside. Obviously, she never did. I guess she wasn't as unique as Lazarus as I thought.

That was another good reason why I wanted to die spiritually. I ultimately believed every Word in the Bible and prayed that my grandmother would live to be one hundred years old. Therefore, I waited for her to rise again. If God did it then, he could do it now, right? Even at the cemetery, her casket was not sealed entirely, and I thought, 'This is it; she is about to get up. She is so dramatic.' I sat there anticipating, listening for her voice, waiting for her to rise.

She never did. I even went to the cemetery a week later to see if the ground was disturbed. It was rock solid. So, yes, a good spiritual death seemed the most logical thing for me to do. After all, it seemed that every minister I knew had lied. I prayed, and God did not answer. I believed, and it was for nothing. Therefore,

I chose to commit spiritual suicide. After all, I could commit this deadly act and hide the evidence. Who would know, as we were collectively isolated?

I felt less like a child and more like an orphan during that time. I believed God abandoned me and left me on Satan's doorstep with a note reading, 'take the worst care of her' simply because I thought God was not listening to me. For years, I thought I had what I called God's ear. He would talk, and I would listen. The year I became a minister, ironically, the same year my grandmother died, I spoke at least four times within a few months. That was quite unusual because most ministers in my church preached that much during an entire year. However, God was speaking to me. I remembered two messages about the Holy Ghost and the church being on one accord. God was speaking, but I took it upon myself to interpret what he was saying.

When I spoke my "Thus says the Lord" sermon concerning the power of being on one accord, I earnestly believed it had to do with the church coming together to witness God's healing power for my grandmother. Why else would God want the church to be of one mind and one spirit? I preached that sermon enthusiastically, excited about what God had intended to do. He had healed my grandmother so many times, and I was confident that he would recover her again. So, when she died, I was perplexed and angry with God. I didn't understand why he would call the church to unity if he were ultimately going to call our leader home.

It didn't make sense to me, so my anger only increased. I felt used by God. However, not in the way that many of us think, more like being manipulated by him. God spoke, I answered, I obeyed, and he turned around and did the exact opposite. I no longer had God's ear; even if I did, I didn't want it anymore. If he was speaking, I wasn't listening.

I hadn't heard from God in months, and I was okay with it. Or perhaps he was talking to me, and I no longer knew his voice. Either way, it didn't matter. I was done, ready to eulogize my spiritual man. *You were a good man; you followed your course and did your best, but now's time to say goodbye.*

INTRODUCTION

However, stubbornly my spiritual man would not die. It was on life support, and I could not pull the plug. No matter how much I deprived him of God's Spirit, he would not easily succumb to death. Even though I didn't pick up a bible for months, the Word was still in me, alive and active. No matter what sins I tried to commit, the Word would not allow me to backslide completely. I honestly wanted to die spiritually, but the Word kept me alive. It would not allow me to entirely exterminate that part of who I am.

If you are like me, there have been times in which you have been angry with God for one reason or another. I know it is hard to admit, as I cringe at the idea. However, there are times when God's will does not co-exist with our expectations. Therefore we become enraged by disappointments or unanswered prayers, occasionally causing us to want to give up our spiritual race. However, God's hands are upon the righteous, and there is no escape from his grasp. We can try, but we can't run forever.

Trust me, God's legs are longer, and his reach is more expansive than ours. I tried to outrun God for years, but he is the ultimate track star. I was only fooling myself into thinking I could unleash his grip. Yet, he is stronger and exceedingly more robust. Ultimately, I gave up running and did a brisk jog instead.

It's hilarious how I thought I could trick God into thinking I wasn't trying to escape my God-given identity. I followed the commandments, was a faithful steward, and did my duty as a youth leader, but I didn't want to give a total yes. So, instead of running, I did a light jog. I half-heartedly did everything required, yet I was not ready to fall on my sword and completely surrender to God.

My spiritual man was resurrected, but he had to conquer my heart and transform my mind. Therefore, I finally realized spiritually running is just as exhausting as sprints or suicides. So, instead of running, I gave up and decided to walk with God, leading to standing still to recognize the salvation of the Lord.

Through my experiences, I learned who God is, but most importantly, I knew who I was in him. As a youth, God was setting me apart to be different. I never understood why, but I believe it is for a time like this. God needs me to be other than the traditional standard of what we consider holy and be holy individually in him. With my grandmother, God humbled me. He established himself in my life by rebuilding my identity as a child of God. I have God's ear again and have realized that I must speak what God says and not attempt to decipher the meaning. God was telling the church to become unified because our leader would be called home in a few months, and he needed us to be strong, on one accord.

Redeveloping my relationship with God, I started thinking about who God is. During those times in my life, God was my guide, leader, and strength. God is still those things to me. However, he is also my provider, protector, and teacher. I remember hearing the story about Moses and the burning bush as a young child. I should have been amazed by the enflamed tree. However, I was more in awe of God's name, "I Am that I Am."

I didn't quite understand the implications of this name. I just thought God is dope. Who gives their reputation as a cliff-hanger? He just left his name as a fill-in-the-blank, multiple-choice selection, short answer solution for whatever we need him to be. Therefore, God is everything to me; ironically, somehow, I am everything to God.

God's name, I Am, seems to encompass his real character as he can be everything we need. It's impossible to limit God to one specific name or the hundreds of words we call him. God is Elohim, the Creator, as he is El Shaddai, the Almighty God. However, isn't God more than just the originator of life and a mighty being?

He is also Jehovah Jireh, our provider, and Jehovah Rapha, our healer. Yet again, God is more than the supplier of our needs and a physician. God is all, and his name, I Am, signifies his complete identity as being everything to his people. Even with the several names he possesses, I Am that I Am is the one that sums up his entire character. It explains who God is to his people. Each individual on Earth is unique, and special situations and distinctive challenges come with our uniqueness. Therefore, God stating that "he will be what he will be" means that God has us covered no matter our life obstacles.

INTRODUCTION

As I continued to study my favorite name of God, I realized that Jesus also is known as "I am." Jesus would have this name because he is the Son of God. Just like we have surnames representing our genealogy, the deity of God, the Father, and Son, is no different. Since Jesus is the Son of God, it is only natural that he would also use his Father's name. In John's gospel, Jesus used his name, "I am," on seven other occasions.

"I am the Bread of Life" (6:35)

"I am the Light of the world (8:12)

"I am the Door" (10:7)

"I am the Good Shepherd" (10:11)

"I am the resurrection and the life" (11:25 - 26)

"I am the way, the truth, and the life" (14:6)

"I am the True Vine" (15:1).

Even when Jewish leaders confronted Jesus, he stated, "before Abraham was, I Am (John 8:58). Our Savior understood his identity as he was connected to the Father. Therefore, Jesus proclaiming that he was the, I Am, was him distinguishing the Father-Son relationship between him and God.

Now here is the mind-blowing concept. When Jesus died on the cross, he reconciled our relationship back with the Father. Even though we were undeserving, we became joint heirs with Jesus Christ, meaning we have everything Jesus possesses. I know we don't earnestly believe this; if we did, the entire world would be changed. However, can't we at least believe that we are connected to God, and we can also take on the family name, I am?

Too often, we take on illegitimate titles as, "I'm not" or "I can't", when we are the sons and daughters of God. We have been adopted into his divine family but are unwilling to give up our illegitimate names. Therefore, we cling to terms such as Failure, Disappointment, Useless, and any other title our adversary wants us to possess. Those deficient titles don't align well with our status as King's kids. In fact, it lines up with the Father of this world.

Once we accepted Christ, we changed fathers, ultimately changing our names to receive the title I am, as it is a part of our inheritance. We have the right to the family name, yet what are we saying about ourselves? Are we limiting our victory because of current situations? What evidence are we producing? Too many Christians have identity crises as they don't realize the power in "I am."

It is prophetic and provides the children of God to speak triumphantly about who they are in him. God has given us the authority to use his name, "I am, " boldly and confidently. We declare that we are God's children, yet we fail to use "I am" with complete certainty. How powerful would our lives be if we fearlessly proclaim the many things God says we are?

This book is the first of three designed to help you understand who God says you are and who you are in Christ. The last book aims to improve your outlook and understand your Christian identity. Both God and Jesus self-assuredly proclaimed their names because they knew themselves. God is a self-sufficient God, and Jesus is the Christ. They knew they could make these bold affirmations because they knew their influential power. Therefore, we must achieve this same awareness as God's children. Limitations no longer exist because we are taking on the family name. God is; therefore, I am.

Chapter 1

I am a Child of God.

"For ye are all the children of God by faith in Christ Jesus."
—Galatians 3:26

When I look in the mirror, I see an attractive woman for the most part. However, when the lights turn on, the picture fades into an overweight female, hiding gray hairs and bald spots under wigs, with no more than ten eyelashes collectively. My chestnut skin is blotched with childhood memories that look like a connect-the-dots sheet. My once-perfect teeth hold on for dear life, while the others were tossed aside by a dental assistant. Thankfully, I can hide my toothless grin behind these pandemic masks, my bald eyelashes with falsies, and my thinning hair with a full lace closure wig.

I'm far from the ugliest person in the room. In fact, on a good day, I rank slightly above average on the attractive scale. I just need a little foundation, a bit of gloss, a few contouring shades, and VOILA! However, no one knows that deep down, I feel like my looks are fading without marriage prospects, a boyfriend, a suitor, nothing. At this point, I almost feel like I would take being someone's mistress because my only companion is Sammie, my Yorkie

Terrier. I love my little man, but he can't tell me I am beautiful on those days when I resemble an old hag.

Then it's my living conditions. First, let me say that I am grateful for my home. It's a small countryside bungalow that I gutted and designed during the "flip my house" era. I love my archways and the openness of the house. I love that I can position myself in one place and see every room. I just have to ensure I don't stand on a soft spot.

Yeah, my wooden floors are fragile, probably due to poor plumbing issues. Most days, I am greeted with the cesspool's outdoor fragrance, and sometimes, I feel I can smell it seeping through the floors. Thousands of dollars have gone into paying for that by my mother. Obviously, I can't afford it with a mountain of financial aid, a teacher's salary, and a hopeless doctorate's degree that I think would gather more use as a dustpan.

Next, let's venture to talk about my career. Despite having degrees in child and adolescent behaviors, I listen to my co-workers' daily struggles with student behavioral problems. Not a day goes by that one of our lovely students is sent to the office for a violation of the infamous triple D's: disrespect, disruption, or defiance. October me would generally attempt to de-escalate the problems. After all, I studied child and adolescent behaviors for half my life, as I am a mental health therapist first and a teacher second. If that's not enough, I've had clients draw knives at me, and I'm still here to tell the story. So, I think that alone qualifies me to deal with our little band of juvenile delinquents.

However, no one listens. The veteran teachers are esteemed veterans who I feel see me as having less knowledge, and the new teachers are so green that they stand out in our coloring box. So, April me sits there listening to the yelling, the screaming, and empty lectures that fall on deaf ears.

Many days, I sit and wonder, *why am I here*? I love teaching; however, I keep wondering if this is all life has to offer me. I've applied for numerous jobs at the college level and have been denied. I even applied for the behavioral specialist position in my school district as I was believed to be a forerunner. I was the last in the pack as I worked alongside the hired gentleman. Don't get me wrong. He is qualified, *even* if his wife did hire him.

Then in every school meeting, I have to suffer through the accolades of a co-worker who the poverty-stricken families call "The Great White Hope." I think I will pull my weave if I have to listen once more about how great she is with student behaviors. She is definitely outstanding with relationships. One of the best, but anyone is good with student behaviors if coddling without correction is done. They are even better with behaviors if they hand out money to the poor Black families in our community. They can even gain a noble peace prize for co-dependency. Again, don't get me wrong. She truly cares for the students. I just believe that being good with behaviors goes beyond picking up 3rd graders, wrapping them up as babies, and having them make cooing sounds. I have learned to smile with my eyes and scowl under my mask.

Maybe it's jealousy. Maybe. Or, possibly, I wanted recognition for myself and others who work just as hard. Perhaps I may need some validation. Or it could be that I feel like I am still lacking despite my education, looks, and intelligence. These are my inner thoughts as I drag through life, and I constantly have to remind myself that no matter what, I am still a child of God.

I would be amiss if I didn't say this helps me most days, but not all. At times I feel like my confession does not match my status. Like I have come immune to the fact that I am a child of the highest governing authority in Heaven and Earth. My looks don't resemble royalty, and my bank account is far from it. Nevertheless, I am still a child of God with a worthless degree, gray hairs, and back fat decorated by stretch marks.

Perhaps my declaration lacks confidence because everyone seems to think they are children of God. You would think so, looking at how sinners are blessed. They have their mansions, cosmetic surgery, and fame, but I remind myself that they don't have the benefits of being a part of this royal family. They are merely his Creation and not children, meaning they serve little use. I know that sounds extremely harsh, but a creator has intentions for their creation. Why would God be any different? He created man to praise, worship, and do good works. If this is not happening, then they are useless. God wants his creation to become his children ultimately. Until this happens, we are merely worthless bastards.

Now, I would never call anyone a bastard. I am merely restating what Apostle Paul said (Heb 8:12). Please don't shoot the messenger. Paul said it, and I am simply the tool repeating his sentiments. He just believed that people who did not want to adhere to God's teachings were illegitimate, born out of unholy matrimony. Therefore, those who accept God are called his children, while those who deny him are seen as bastards. Again, Paul said it, not me.

However, I will say that it appears that unbelievers, those so-called bastards, believe they are God's children more than those he is called. Most of the world claims this name without claiming the requirements of the title. We have taken up our cross and denied ourselves to follow behind Christ, yet we wholeheartedly don't believe we are God's children. We say we are but have not fully grasped what that means.

Every year, I would watch the music awards to see my favorite singers and rappers take the stage to give their acceptance speeches. And everyone would acknowledge God every time, referencing him as "The Big Man upstairs." Then, in the same breath, some would throw up gang signs while loud beeps would replace four-letter words. Then the others would return to perform their latest hits that focused on sex, drugs, and getting money illegally. Ironically, they also believed they were God's children. Perhaps, maybe they are the black sheep of the family?

If they can willfully sin and recognize they are the children of God, then what about his rightful heirs? We, as Christians, must know we are the heirs to the Kingdom, the chosen people, the royal priesthood, the holy nation (1 Pet 2:9). The truth is that most Christians know this scripture, they will even cite it, but only a handful honestly believe it. We proclaim to be offsprings of the Almighty; however, our thoughts, disposition, and behaviors tend not to align with our royal positioning. Instead of acting like high-born nobles, we slothfully shuffle around like underprivileged servants when our Father is the King.

God commands us to be of good cheer and courage. He is our provider and the supplier of all our needs. The unfortunate truth is that we forget that along the way. We become overwhelmed by our current situations that it clogs our minds with financial obligations versus liberating our hearts to trust God. God is a good father despite us being unruly children. Maybe, that's why we lack trust in him because we are plagued by our unwillingness to follow him fully. Or, perhaps we lack faith because are problems look larger than an enormous God. The bottom line is that we are God's children, whom he delights in giving provisions. Regrettably, we are troubled by our existing problems because we look outwardly versus inwardly.

On the surface, we are surrounded by problems. Once we get out of one issue, other problematic situations take their place. We we will suffer because Christ did, but heartache is not the only part of our Christianity. In God is fullness of joy despite our circumstances being a bucket full of tears. That is merely what occurs on the outside. However, internally, Christians should possess joy and peace when facing life's challenges. We have the indwelling of the Holy Spirit, which means God is with us every second of our day. Even unconscious, God watches, makes provisions, and fights on our behalf. We must take heart in knowing that our Father is with us when problems arise. He is there, willing and capable of taking care of his children.

No one dares to harm Arian; she's my daughter, and it's my warrior princess instinct to protect her by any means necessary. She is currently of age to defend herself. However, I am her mother, a fearless lioness. No matter how old she gets, I will be there, ready to lay the smackdown on anyone who even thinks of harming her. I've scared many boyfriends with just one look, pulled my hair back, taken earrings off, and had Vaseline ready to go with a few choice friends. With an eye glare and a head shake, I have scared a five-year-old who teased her on the school bus. Again, no one messes with my daughter, and with all of my antics, God is still infinitely greater at coming to our rescue.

God is a father that protects and provides. No matter how spiritually mature we get or how naturally wealthy we may be, God still delights in being a protector and a provider for his children. Matthew 7:11 proclaims that we still do good things for our children, despite us being evil. I never considered myself wicked, but I still provided for my daughter despite my sins. Even though I am a mere human, subjected to minimum finances and failure, she lacked nothing. However, our spiritual father is the Creator of wealth and life's sustainer. Since I was evil and could provide every toy, latest electronic gadget, trips to Europe, and name-brand fashion for my daughter, how much more will a righteous God give to his children?

We limit our status as children of God because of our inability to recognize ourselves as his. God boldly proclaims that we are his children, yet we tend to focus more on ourselves and less on him. I believe that the self is the destroyer of being a child of God. Most of God's offspring encounter low self-worth and self-esteem. An omnipotent, self-sufficient God calls us his children, yet we tend to think lowly of ourselves and cannot recognize our value within his Kingdom.

Dwelling on ourselves will cause us to lose sight of our God-given character as his child. Our self-identity should be so entangled in God that there is no room for it. I know this is the pinnacle of the Christian life that many may never obtain. However, if we could let go of ourselves and hold fast to God's identity as our Father, we would finally recognize that we are more exceptional than others.

I know that saying we are superior to unbelievers appears to be prideful boasting. Yet, I believe Christians live too far left on the spectrum of meek and humble than extraordinary. If we could fully immerse ourselves into being God's children, then I believe that the trajectory of our lives would change. No longer would self-doubt stop us from fulfilling our youthful ambitions. The power of God would contain murderous insecurities, and our self-esteem would no longer be violated because we know who we are as God's elect. Unquestionably, our confidence would increase, becoming more assertive and Godly-assured in our identity. Even scriptures and biblical promises would take on new meaning because we would shift from mere declarations to the actual belief, knowing that we possess greater (1 John 4:4).

We are more significant because greater lives inside of us. Yet, is this the image we show the world? The regrettable truth is that many of God's children look more defeated than victorious. Why would the world want to follow us when we look trodden down by life? Our lives should be what propels men and women to Christ.

Unbelievers can see past our scripture quoting and look directly at our lives. They know scriptures just as well as we do, but they need to see them exhibited through the children of God. There is no point in saying, "God will supply all our needs according to his riches in glory," when we are always in need. That's the picture we paint. Unbelievers are looking at what we show versus what we say. Are we demonstrating that we are the children of God, or do we look more like begging orphans?

You can't recognize your greatness if you stifle God's. Your Father reigns supreme over every disease, financial account, familial issue, and anything that could interrupt your sanity. Do you know that God is more significant, more substantial, and bigger than everything in your life? Unfortunately, you cannot understand your significance if you limit God's. It's time to realize who's your Daddy.

WHO IS GOD OUR FATHER?

If we could take a moment to answer this question, it may lead to a greater spiritual understanding of who we are as the children of God. Ironically, it is challenging to summarize God into one clear definition. Perhaps, this is why we do not fully understand the benefits we possess as God's children.

God is the highest presiding government within the universe, the Self-sufficient Supreme Being and Ruler of *everything*.

He reigns in power, loving-kindness, and divine understanding. God is almighty, everlasting, incomparable, unchanging, and never failing. His mercy is infinite, his character is loving, and he is faithful and just, willing to forgive all our sins. Therefore, being greater has nothing to do with us but has everything to do with our Father being who he is.

It's incomprehensible to think that the Supreme Ruler of all the universe claims us to be his children. It's even more mind-boggling that we cannot comprehend the benefits we hold. In the financial world, there is a saying that says, "leaving money on the table," which means missing opportunities for financial gain. As Christians, we miss great benefits when we cannot fully comprehend what it means to be a child of God. God does not limit us as children, but we restrict his ability as our Father. If we could think of our natural fathers as the most important man in the world, then maybe we could tangibly understand what it means to be a child of the King.

Let's consider if our natural fathers were the wealthiest, the most influential man among the seven continents. We would want for absolutely nothing. Imagine living in hundred-million-dollar mansions while coasting around Ibiza on a six-hundred-million-dollar yacht. What about taking two hundred thousand dollar trips to outer space or roaming around Abu Dhabi in a three-million-dollar Ferrari Pininfarina Sergi? A three hundred thousand dollar golden bathroom could be ours for the asking. It seems like a fantastic fantasy; however, this is a poor man's comparison to what it means to be a child of God.

Why settle for a golden toilet when God promised we would walk on golden streets? The job of a commode is to dispense waste to the sewer, while roads are made to travel to unperceived destinations. Hilariously, all urine and feces will travel the same way, whether you have a golden encrusted toilet or a plastic pot. However, God provides us with golden highways that lead to further riches beyond our imaginations versus wasteful opportunities that travel to the sewer.

Unfortunately, we are so absorbed in worldly riches that we forget that our inheritance is stored in Heaven. What are a trillion dollars to God when he owns the entire universe? Our Father owns everything and even has power over life and death.

Think about it. Regardless of how much money anyone possesses, even the wealthiest man will one day succumb to death. However, as God's children, he gives us everlasting life. No money in all the world can preserve life as no amount of wealth can persuade God to provide us with a second one. Gratefully, as the children of God, we have this treasure that no man can buy. We are heirs of the resurrection. Worldly possessions are great, but our Father's spiritual blessings are abundant.

As the children of God, we must not become discouraged by the things we can see but take on courage for the things we cannot. In John 14: 1 – 3, Jesus says that He goes to prepare a place for us within the Father's house. Our imaginations are not equipped to comprehend God's mansion. Some have tried to imitate it, but it's not duplicated. I've seen pictures replicating Heaven. Beautiful as they were, it is nothing compared to what God has prepared for his children.

Sure, I wouldn't mind having a Mercedes-Benz Maybach Exelero parked in a four-garaged home overlooking the Atlantic. At this point, I would settle for a Tesla with the gas prices as they are. However, my incorruptible treasures are left at home in Heaven, being watched over by the best security system. Even with the rising gas prices, God allows me to fill up my 28-gallon tank, which is over ten percent of my salary. Therefore, we should rejoice in knowing that "no eye has seen, no ear has heard, and no mind has imagined the things that God has prepared for those who love him" (1 Cor 2:9 ISV).

We have not witnessed our heavenly blessings yet, but we can rejoice in the tangible allowances God provides here on Earth. Our Father offers numerous immediate benefits. As the elect of God, we are blessed with healing, provision, forgiveness, and salvation. These blessings are readily available because we are children of the Almighty God. Each of our Father's benefits improves our standing in him to reach our full potential as King's kids and form a perfect relationship with him.

WE ARE LOADED WITH BENEFITS

The Benefit of Power

One morning, a student was escorted to my class because he was visibly upset. He wouldn't tell anyone what was wrong because no one could do anything. Trying to make light of the situation, I jokingly told him he didn't know what power I possessed. He took his chances and revealed his father was facing a lengthy prison sentence on his way to court. He was absolutely right; I had no judiciary connections to stop the hands of justice, and even if I did, I wasn't about to get involved. Without thinking, I quickly prayed that God would fix the situation. The next day, the student enthusiastically exclaimed that his father's case was rescheduled and his sentence would likely be reduced from several years to a few months.

As the children of God, we are endowed with authority over life's circumstances. Even in the situation with my student, I was thinking of my own influence as a teacher without realizing my power as God's elect. God has equipped us with his Spirit that produces wisdom, knowledge, and understanding beyond mere learning for everyday living (1 Cor 12:4 – 11). As the omniscient God, he provides insight into the past, current intelligence, and future awareness to help guide and direct our paths. This knowledge allows us to make better decisions to avoid life's roadblocks and delays. We merely need to understand that we can handle every situation because God gives us the authority and power as his children.

One of God's best gifts was creating his children in his image through inducing us with the Holy Spirit. God created man in his image, but the mere fact is that some of God's creation is more powerful simply because they have the spirit of God dwelling in them. Every living creature has God's breath because they are alive, yet those who have the Spirit of God benefit from spiritual power, which provides a more abundant life.

Our lives are more enriched because of this God-given ability through our Father. We are endowed with the spiritual seed of the Holy Ghost, which means that God blesses us with the same power He gave to Jesus and the disciples. Peter healed the sick (Acts 5:15), Paul removed demons and raised the dead (Acts 16:18; Acts 20:8 – 12), and Stephen and Philip performed great signs and wonders (Acts 6:8; 8:6 – 8). The same power is still active and alive in the children of God. We simply need to move from proclamation to activation.

The Benefit of Access

It's peculiar that we are directly connected to a holy and wise God. It seems implausible in our lowly state; we can talk to the Creator and Ruler of the world, and most importantly, he answers. At the very least, it seems we should have an appointment or prepare ourselves for audience with the King. It would be absurd to think I could just ring the doorbell at 1600 Pennsylvania Avenue and ask to speak to the Commander and Chief, especially ill-attired. Nevertheless, God only requires us to speak, and he, in turn, listens every time.

With Jesus's death, the veil was ripped, decreasing the separation from God and his children. The curtain's significance demonstrated God's holiness and unapproachability during the old testament. Only the high priests were permitted to atone for sin by entering the Holy of Holies. Even then, sacrificial Blood was sprinkled to prevent their deaths as no man has lived and seen God (Ex 33:20). However, God ripped the cloth in two, establishing the new covenant, in which there is no more division between God and his children.

Tearing the veil allowed God's children to have a closer, more intimate relationship with him through prayer. It is safe to say that God had a close bond with the Old Testament patriarchs. However, our connection should be more remarkable because 1) we have God dwelling on the inside, and 2) we have the power to pray in the name of Jesus (John 14:13–14).

When I referenced these scriptures, the word became alive for me. I've always prayed in Jesus's name. However, my actions are transforming into beliefs. God clearly stated that I could ask *anything* in his Son's name, and he would do it. There was no maybe or stuttering involved. The Almighty God, who cannot lie, said he would perform what I asked. I invite you, as I did, to immediately stop reading and start praying, as *every* request that is sealed in Jesus's name, which does not counteract his plan, will be granted.

Jesus's death and his name activated our greatest weapon, prayer. Nevertheless, it is often our worst setback. Establishing a prayer life helps God's children connect to him through praise, worship, supplication, intercession, and thanksgiving. Neglecting to pray is the same as laying down one of our spiritual weapons. Our prayers reach and move God to work on our behalf. We should never overlook the benefit of access as it comes with the cost of our Savior's Blood. Having a prayer life gives us the gift of fellowship and ushers us into the presence of God. Yet, as believers, we discount our bond with the Father when we fail to pray, neglecting the attached benefits of restoration, provision, and forgiveness. God is waiting to hear our requests, but he will answer them most of all.

The Benefit of Love

As a child of God, we have the reassurance that a perfect being loves us. There was no greater love than when God sacrificed his beloved Son for this world. It might not seem like much as John 3:16 has been commercialized. However, think of it like this. Would we kill our child to adopt a wicked, unruly one? Then, have the adopted child ungratefully deny our existence despite our unconditional care and love towards them daily? Ironically, this is what God did. He sacrificed his perfect Son to adopt faulty, damaged children because of his divine love.

I AM A CHILD OF GOD.

God loved us so much that he took pleasure in Jesus's suffering (Isa 53:10). Let's think about this for a minute. Jesus was accused of blasphemy, arrested, and humiliated. The Roman soldiers stripped him naked before men. He was flogged with a leather whip entangled with sharp material carving his flesh from his bones, making his entire body an open wound. They whipped him thirty-nine times as forty could have killed him. They gave him a crown of thorns, hammering it over his head until it penetrated his skin, skull, and brain. After his body was weakened by sleep deprivation, blood loss, and traveling the road to Golgotha with the world's weight on his shoulders, they crucified him. His bodyweight began to crush his lungs as they continually inflicted insults, mockery, and emotional damage. The worst appears that God abandoned him in his hours of need and, most of all, *delighted* in his misery (Isa 53:10)

I understand the meaning behind Jesus's death as it was God's goodwill to provide the guilt offering through his Son. However, I was slightly astonished that Isaiah said it *pleased* God. Pleased seems such a happy word to describe such a sullen occasion. Yet, God was satisfied with his Son's torture for our sake. His love for us was demonstrated through Jesus Christ's death. God gave up what he loved most, so he could become a Father to us all. I believe that John said it best, "See what great love the Father has lavished on us, that we should be called children of God! And that is what we are! The reason the world does not know us is that it did not know him" (1 John 3:1, NIV).

God's love goes beyond merit, bloodlines, or infatuations, as his love is perfect because he is divinely flawless. Our imperfections should omit us from even being associated with God, let alone his children. Nevertheless, God sees worth in his creation, and conceivably this is why the world disregards believers because they don't see the resemblance of our Father. Yet, regardless of our character flaws and shortcomings, God not only loves unconditionally but calls us sons and daughters.

God's redemption plan to restore creation to children was the best love story ever told. Satan was the ultimate villain entrapping

God's creation in webs of sin, dooming them to eternal death. They were slaves to his devices and chained to live in darkness forever. However, the protagonist, God, slays the dragon by sacrificing what he loves because he, in turn, loves us. After his victorious rescue, God crowns us with compassion and heals our diseases. He lavishes us with forgiveness, mercy, and grace while adopting us into his royal family, changing our names from his creation to his children. How wonderful to know that this is not a fairy tale or some fable but truthful accounts that God provides to live eternally "happily ever after."

Every I am statement is only done by our affirmation of being a child of the King. Therefore, when any obstacle or self-doubt penetrates our minds, remember that we are children of God. We have been adopted and appointed by our heavenly Father, who allows us to walk in the highest of places (Hab 3:19). Therefore, we should never feel worthless or dismayed. Our Father is God, the almighty being of this universe, who has accepted and adopted us into his royal family.

His arms are open wide, ready to accept us as his children. We will no longer have to doubt his unconditional love beyond merits. It is unwavering and unmovable. Although we've experienced past hurts, God's affection towards us is more incredible than any rejections we have ever suffered. He is our heavenly Father that waits patiently to reconcile our relationship. He is the Father who always listens, provides, and protects. He never stops caring about us. These are the benefits of claiming God to be our Father. Accepting him allows us to take on his characteristics of love, joy, happiness, and peace. Our actions will align with our Father's, and we can take on God's name; I am, because we are his.

Chapter 2

I am God's treasure.

> "For you are a people holy to the Lord your God. The Lord, your God, has chosen you to be a people for his treasured possession, out of all the people who are on the face of the Earth."
>
> —Deuteronomy 7:6 ESV

ONCE I HEARD A story about a wealthy woman who had misplaced a piece of jewelry. She had several other valuables yet; she frantically searched for this one. Her friends were puzzled as to why she would eagerly hunt for this piece. After all, it wasn't a family heirloom nor one of her most prized possessions. The jewelry could easily be replaced. Nevertheless, she understood that it did not lose its value despite being lost.

Throughout my ordeals, I have learned that no matter how far I am disoriented in a forest of despair, I do not lose my worth to God. Admittedly, there have been times in my life when I have felt more misplaced than found. It seemed I was wandering in existence, aimlessly trying to find my purpose. I repeatedly missed the mark as life was a vast wilderness with rocky shores, rushing rivers, and dangerous paths. It was hard to find my way out of the thicket, feeling like I was abandoned in life's jungle, despite feeling lost, God never gave up on my Hide and Go Seek game. God always found a way to see me in the middle of my chaos.

Failure had become an undesired friend throughout my life. My successes were few, and my disappointments always reminded me I was inadequate. Graduating early from college should have been a win, but my first job was close to minimum wage. My current job wasn't much better, especially since my school district decided to pay me like a long-term sub while seeking my provisional licenses.

One hundred dollars a day, almost the same amount I made twenty years ago. That daily allowance was even less than that, as Uncle Sam had to get his cut. The hiring signs at local fast-food restaurants looked more appealing daily.

All my life, I worked hard to pursue higher education. I thought I would become comfortably wealthy, nothing extravagant, just upper middle class, making six figures. That was my dream. However, let's just say education is overrated. Don't get me wrong, I think education is excellent, but I have spent hundreds of dollars decorating my living room wall with expensive framed degrees, in which I wish I had kept the receipt for those frames. At least I could have used that money for a much-needed new refrigerator. However, I had to buy elaborate frames for elaborate degrees that were as elaborately useless as I felt.

Even social media influencers, who hadn't finished high school yet, made the equivalent of my student loans one hundred times over. No degrees, just fame and wealth. I think it's a cardinal sin to become an influencer at my age. I am too old and holy to create an Only Fans account. I don't have the patience to develop how-to-do videos, and I'm too dull to go viral. Even one of my students hilariously advised me to sell my feet on eBay. The following week, I got a pedicure noticing that someone paid off their student loans this way. All my life, I've lived by the slogan, *the more you know, the further you go*. NBC lied because I learned a lot but wasn't going anywhere.

I've literally become immune to rejection letters. When I see them, I am grateful. At least those agencies had the decency to tell

I AM GOD'S TREASURE.

me I'm not qualified versus not even bothering to dignify me with an email. One time, I got a rejection letter from a publisher who specifically addressed me by name and read my proposal. I was so thankful I emailed her back for the rejection like she had offered me a six-digit advance. When my first book was published, I thought it was a colossal joke or a clever scam. Yet, it was an actual publisher, and even with that win, I still felt like a loser.

Perhaps I have failed so many times that I could not recognize that I had succeeded. I had a doctorate, which equaled a meager salary and position. I was attractive, yet my last relationship was roughly ten years ago with a guy that lived hundreds of miles away. God called me, but I felt powerless and hopeless even then. My self-worth was meaningless as broken glass, and I was too deep inside the rabbit hole to be found.

Ironically, like the woman who searched for her jewelry, God saw my purposeless pursuit, rescuing me because of my importance to him. Often, I wonder what's brewing on my surface that God found worth saving. I've failed him more than I rather admit. I sinned more than I care to count, but he continues to see me, even when I misplace myself.

In 2013, I chose to go on a Kenya mission with several church leaders, and I was the least of them. Pastors, elders, and ministers of the gospel were on this mission, and I was going because my father started it. So, I thought.

I was knocked to the floor; no sooner did those ideas enter my mind. My face was buried on a grimy surface, being rebuked by the voice of God. I was clearly having a Damascus moment, as I was blinded by my own beliefs when God had predestined me for that trip. With a tear-stained face, I realized that God found me valuable regardless of how I felt about myself.

I still wondered why God desired me on this task in the weeks leading to the trip. He had a purpose for me to be there, but why? I know God wasn't having a senior moment, but it didn't make sense why he chose me over others with more value.

At that time, I wasn't a preacher; I didn't have any spiritual gifts that would be specifically needed to aid the mission. I was a youth leader and a poor excuse for one at that. I loved working with our young people, but I wasn't particularly trying to knock on doors to find more. Nor was I willing to give up my weekends to keep them Godly motivated. I did the bare minimum, choir rehearsals, summer bible school, and occasionally helped my mom with a youth grant. These so-called acts could not possibly qualify me for traveling halfway around the world. Maybe to another city, but not another continent. If it wasn't that, then what was it? I had no idea but doubtfully loaded up a suitcase full of candy, crayons, and coloring books to head thousands of miles to the Motherland.

Arriving at the village, I tried hard to hold back tears as I repeatedly repented. Mainly because of my doubt in both my fathers. In 2007, while my parents started preparing for their vacation to Kenya, my father revealed that God showed him eight men on a beach. Ironically, in rare forms, my father would need to witness to them. My father is the ultimate evangelist. He is the one that goes to Disney World and wonders if Mickey is saved. However, this was not the happiest place on Earth, and the gatekeepers didn't have metal detectors but AK-47s. Of course, we tried to talk him against it, primarily since this was a foreign land and his brother told us the dangers he encountered while smuggling a bible to specific places in Asia. However, my father was determined, and from that vacation came a congregation, which made me question even more why God chose me to be there.

My next private altar call occurred when I saw the children. As we were ushered to the front of the congregation, I peered over to see several little ones enclosed in a building. There were so many of them. As I listened to the energetic message from the pastor, who happened to be one of the beach boys my father met years ago, I kept feeling a notion of heading toward them. It felt like a magnetic force was pulling me in that direction. Strangely enough, it appeared my crippling social anxiety was gone as I roamed the small African village to see the children. A tear did fall from my eyes as I realized that God saw value in me, and those children helped me find my worth.

It's amazing how God will use situations and events in our lives to show us who we are. As it turns out, I was not a poor excuse for a youth leader as I thought. Those children didn't know anything about my past failures or how meaningless I felt. They only saw a woman who cared enough to bring goodie bags but also fell in love with them. God had revealed what I couldn't see. It wasn't about how much I did for God but how I did it. With most of my commitments, I did them out of love and service. God had to show me; it only took traveling thousands of miles away from home to get the hint.

Even though I thought I was lost to God, it appeared that I had misplaced myself. Incredibly, we are too valuable to God for him to lose sight of his children. We lose ourselves in past hurts and failures, which handicaps our thinking to feel as if we are useless or worthless. Yet, we are valuable to God. I could not see my use to him simply because the voices inside my head told me what I was not.

I am not stupid.

I am not worthless.

I am good.

Unfortunately, I've believed the worse about myself, so much that it was inconceivable that God would see the best.

That's the foundation of our harmful self-image. We allow negative, destructive thoughts to damage our worth when God has found us worthwhile. A child of God is like a magnificent piece of jewelry in a thrift store. We may get ignored as no one knows our value until they look at the price tag. Our price tag is sealed with the Blood of Jesus, purchased and redeemed. Therefore, as the children of God, his prized possessions, we cannot allow negative thoughts to cloud our mirrors. We must use our spiritual Windex to remove the stains of negativity and see what God sees.

When God looks at us, he does not see failure; he sees worth. We are God's exclusive trophy, his prized treasure (Deut 14:2, 1 Pet 2:9). We may not feel like a diamond in the rough, but we are the fairest gems in all the land. Nothing in God's eye pales in comparison to how precious we are to him. We are loved and honored in his sight (Isa 43:4). Therefore, we are more beautiful than opal, more radiant than emerald. We are the glory of God, the rarest of all jewels (Rev 21:11). If this is the case, you are probably asking yourself, "why do I feel like cheap cubic zirconia?"

We feel like artificial diamonds because our adversary wants us to feel ill-equipped and synthetic, like an imitation diamond at Tiffany's, having no place, unqualified and ill-manufactured. Also, let's not forget that Satan once was in good standing with God, but now he wants to magnify our flaws when God designed us to be flawless in him. God honored Satan by covering him in these gems when he created topaz, diamonds, onyx, jasper, gold, and sardius (Ezek 28:13). However, once he became self-righteous and prideful, he lost his standing with God. Ironically, Satan knows our value, yet he deceives us into thinking we're worthless pieces of hardened plastic versus radiant gemstones.

How can we be ill-manufactured when the best jeweler has created us? We were made by the hands of God to be precious jewels and not cheap glass posing as something we are not. We are God's golden treasure, not discounted materials turning fingers green. We are the real deal. We aren't gold plated; we're 24 Karat.

Unfortunately, that is the picture that Satan paints. Our adversary would like nothing more than to dull our radiance. To make us think that we are fake Christians because of our past. Therefore, he reminds us of our raw sinful form; instead of the gems we were made to be.

WE MAY OFTEN LOSE OUR LUSTER, BUT WE HAVE NOT LOST OUR WORTH.

If we can be honest for a moment, every Christian is not the picture of Christianity when they first receive Christ. The truth is that diamonds, in their raw form, look more like rocks than what we would want dangling around our necks. It does not look like much

I AM GOD'S TREASURE.

initially, but miners understand its value. That's how it is once we undergo our making process.

When we look at ourselves, we see a liar, a fornicator, a cheater, a gambler, a money-grubbing robber that is far from being God's treasure. However, God sees past sin's griminess and what he has ordained us to be. He doesn't toss us aside because we have flaws. Instead, God looks past our faults, understands our values, and simply polishes us as his treasure.

No child of God is perfect. No doubt about it, we are defectively flawed children, dirtied by our transgressions, corrupted by sin. Even though we have accepted Christ, we always find a way to mess it up. Sin creeps in, and Satan rears his ugly head to pollute our minds into thinking we are worthless, causing us to move further away from God.

Our adversary does this because he knows our worth better than we do. Still, like the diamond that cannot return to its raw form, neither can we. Let's not fool ourselves; we will fall short at times. However, we don't have to return to the muck. Thankfully, we have the best cleaning solution, the Blood of Jesus Christ, which always washes away our imperfections.

The Blood not only cleans our slate but also rejuvenates our minds. Often, the children of God act like cheap glass versus durable diamonds simply because we allow others to discount our worth. Glass is easily broken, but we, as God's treasure, cannot be quickly shattered. We are the children of the Highest God. The rarest and most stunning jewels in the universe. We cannot be tossed aside like fool's gold, even when we act foolishly. No matter how dirty we have become by failure and sin, we are still diamonds through repentance.

Researching how diamonds are processed, I realized that it is similar to God's designation of us as his treasure. As I said before, diamonds do not look like diamonds, nor more than we tend to look like the treasure of God. However, just like the diamond, we as Christians must undergo a process to ensure that we resemble Christ. Even though we go through the same steps, we have different trials and tribulations that miraculously produce the same quality of worth.

THE PROCESS OF BECOMING A TREASURE OF GOD

Step 1: The Crushing

Diamonds are often found in igneous rocks called kimberlite. For the diamond to be removed, it must first be crushed. The crushing process is delicate as the kimberlite ore must be broken to extract the diamond from the rock. The stone has no value within itself, yet it yields a diamond with greater worth. We may view our lives as mundane or meaningless; however, we are the diamonds in the rough. To be revealed, we must first be crushed.

We view ourselves as valueless because we surround ourselves with pointless pursuits, not allowing God to free us from our kimberlite. When miners crush the ore, it involves extreme pressure. The force helps break the strength of the rock without destroying the diamond. As the treasure of God, we must first be broken from our strongholds for our worth to be revealed. It is often a painful and grueling act, but it must occur to have God remove us from the useless debris that we create. It may not feel good, but there is power in the pressure.

It's natural for us to seek promising careers, fancy homes, and loving relationships. Unfortunately, these things become strongholds as we tend to put them ahead of God, often resulting in dire consequences. God will remove what we loved or built to reveal our worth by first showing his. He wants his treasure to shine with the acknowledgment that his luster allows us to prosper. Therefore, he will crush our spirits until we are utterly broken, totally dependent upon him. Our true treasure is revealed through our brokenness as we learn our success has nothing to do with our capabilities but his.

Step 2: The Screening and the Scrubbing

Once the ore is crushed, it must undergo screening and scrubbing to remove additional excess materials from the diamond. Since the crushing process is strenuous, miners must screen the diamonds to determine if they were able to handle being removed from the kimberlite. Unfortunately, some diamonds are discarded because they cannot survive the crushing procedure. These diamonds were unfit to be used, just like some believers whose faith could not withstand hardship. Unlike the examiners of the diamond, God does not abandon us. We typically are the ones who discard ourselves to re-experience the crushing again until he believes we are strong enough, ensuring that his treasure will last.

As the ore is scrubbed to remove unwanted fine materials, God washes away any continued unrighteousness that will dull our radiance. We can think of this process as being built up in the Spirit. God will break us to rebuild us again, removing those things that are not like him and allowing us to shine even brighter. Even after the ore is crushed, the diamond still has excessive dust and debris hiding its true nature. God will not allow us to be revealed as dirty and unradiant to the world. Instead, after his crushing, he gives us a good scrubbing to ensure that we look like his precious treasure.

Steps 3: Concentration and Collections

First, can I just say how amazed I am by these next steps? I must admit; that sometimes, I feel like I am stretching some of my antics when writing, forcing some things to fit. However, come on, *concentration and collection.* Really? I don't think I even have to explain this process to you. Still nevertheless, after the diamond is washed, it's set apart from the other wasteful materials. Thankfully, God will remove us from the waste.

My garbage was friends. They were good people, and I loved them dearly, yet God was concentrating me for his divine purpose, and everything else around me was trash. Please don't think I am calling my friends garbage. Again, those people were my friends, my ride-or-die. I miss them; however, God knew the treasure he placed inside me was being wasted away. Simply put, I placed friends before God. However, God had to remove me from the wasteful material that I allowed to plague my spirit before he could fully use me.

In short, God is the Miner and the Jeweler. After we have undergone being broken and washed, God will then sanctify us as his treasure and place us to be used for his divine glory. Often we think being set apart is a punishment. However, it is probably one of the highest honors we can have. During this time of separation, God wants to spend time with us as he is jealous for his children. He wants our undivided intention as the lover of our souls, ensuring that we always stay faithful to his purpose.

You have a purpose. After experiencing being broken by God and surviving, there is no way you can deny your worth. You are still standing or, at the very least, sitting. You did not die. You aren't in a corner, sucking your thumb, rocking back and forth in the infant position. Well, are you? Even if you are, GET UP! That's not your purpose. That is not what God intended for your life. I know at times we want to lie in a dark room and succumb to the darkness, but there is a time when we have to realize that we are better than this. That God has better for our lives.

Years ago, a singing group at my church would sing The Williams Brother's song, *My Purpose*. I loved those men because they reminded me of the Five Heartbeats with Eddie Cane included. After I stopped laughing, trying to figure out who Duck, JT, Dresser, and Choir Boy were, I concentrated on the lyrics. The song's lyrics merely asked God to show us our purpose, but most of all, it was a commitment to following through on the plan.

The song speaks to me, and it's a vital prayer that we can use to help determine God's will for our lives. We must ask God to show us our purpose now and then. After being extracted from the ore, the diamond does not know its use until it is revealed. Every diamond is not meant for an engagement ring. Some will find its use in drills, beauty products, or even sound equipment.

Nonetheless, it has value, and its destination was meant for use. We are the treasure of God, designed for great works. However, we cannot stay dormant, sitting in a puddle of tears, without being willing to allow God to show us our purpose.

Our purpose ignites through our gifts and our talents. God has placed these invaluable treasures inside each believer to be used for his divine glory. We may not know those gifts, but it is as simple as determining what you like and what you are good at doing. Me, I love to write. I am not the best writer in the world, but I use this gift to help spread the word of God and encourage others. Perhaps, you may like cooking, then think about starting a soup kitchen in your local community. Or maybe, if you like comic books, start a youth group to create Christian comics. The possibilities are endless, but they only cease to exist when we fail to polish the treasure God has placed inside us.

God requires that his glory is revealed through his children. However, this glory cannot be shown if we fail to start. Remember the parable of the talents (Matt 25:14–30). The servants who used their skills for the Kingdom grew great in God. However, the servant that hid his talent, the gift, was taken away, and he was sent to utter darkness where there was weeping and gnashing of teeth. That sounds pretty extreme, yet our talents are not for us but the edifying of God's Kingdom. When we are too afraid to use what God has given us, we again fail to ignite the flame of his glory, assuring that he shines brightly to the world.

We should not fear sharing our gifts, but we should be afraid if we do not use them. Who wants to be cast away into the darkness because they wouldn't sing, clean, or encourage? I know, I don't. So I will continue to write regardless of how many books I sell. My continued prayer is that if my writing inspires one person, I have done my purpose. Therefore, don't be afraid to start developing your gift as God is with you. Don't forget your humble beginnings as they will lead to a glorious end.

I'M HIDDEN.

We are God's hidden treasure because he sees our worth. Anything that we typically value, we hide. Commonly, we store our valuables in lock boxes, safes, cookie jars, and even under our mattresses to prevent them from being stolen or misplaced. However, God hides us under the shadows of his wings (Ps 17:8). When placed under his shadow, we are never too far away from his presence.

Out of his shadows, we're lost. Yet, God preserves us in the secret places of his tabernacle, in the most intricate areas of his tent (Ps 27:5). Hidden by God means we have safety, security, and protection within his presence. It goes without saying that under his shadows, we are safeguarded. Think about it. What thief is bold enough to steal us away when we are in God's company?

Staying in God's presence ensures that we are covered, but it does not mean we will not go through trials and tribulations. Even diamonds can become damaged. Therefore, we must not think it is strange when we are tested. We are the most durable, hardened gemstones made by God. Our manufacturer knows how resilient we are when trials attempt to decrease our luster. So, he hides us from the problems we cannot stand and allows us to overcome the fiery obstacles we can. Regardless of the difficulties encountered, we are durable enough to stand the test.

Ironically, diamonds can undergo a lot of abuse. They are not easily damaged; they are built to last. In fact, the only thing that can genuinely damage another diamond is another diamond. Here I go again with my stretching antics; however, the only thing that can create a damper in our radiance is another one of God's treasures.

We are God's gems. Sure, some stones shine brighter than others. Yet, we can't become jealous of their luster. In all honesty, we should help boost their glow because we are equally valuable to God. One diamond is beautiful, but a cluster of diamonds is radiant. As the treasure of God, we must stand together before even thinking about putting each other down. Our enemy can't hurt us any more than we can harm each other. Remember, diamonds scratch diamonds, but uplifting all of God's treasure makes us shine brighter.

We must shine. Every one of God's jewels has been equipped to undergo the process that creates them into the finest gemstones. Therefore, God has endowed you with strength, perseverance, and patience to withhold you through life trials. No prosecution can demolish your shine, as no difficulty can damper your glow. You are the invaluable treasure of God. A priceless incorruptible jewel cannot be destroyed as every test is sealed with victory.

You are God's most valuable treasure in all creation, his most prized possession that was made in his image. God values you so much that he places you on a rock called Earth to admire daily. Never will he misplace you, causing you to be lost. You are only lost because you don't understand your worth. You are more precious than the oil in the alabaster box, more beautiful than Solomon's rose of Sharon. Remember, just because you may have lost your luster, it doesn't mean that you have lost your worth.

Chapter 3

I am the righteousness of God.

"For he hath made him to be sin for us, who knew no sin; that we might be made the righteousness of God in him."

—2 Corinthians 5:21

Before we dive into this "I am" statement, I will have to pull every trick in the book to convince you that you are the righteousness of God. I think it was relatively simple to prove that you are his child. It was a welcomed challenge to identify you as God's treasure. However, persuading that you are the righteousness of God will take some divine intervention.

HOLY SPIRIT ACTIVATE.

We are the righteousness of God. There I said it. However, Paul said it first. So, let's start by examining his life. The Apostle Paul said that he was God's righteousness. Comparatively speaking, I think it is safe to say that Paul was the most prominent prosecutor of Christianity. Therefore, how can he even claim to be in good standing with God? We've done some horrific deeds, yet our sinful

I AM THE RIGHTEOUSNESS OF GOD.

actions don't amount to much when considering Paul's persecution against the church.

The Bible does not give a complete account of what violence was issued under Paul's authority. We know he was probably the first prolific serial killer of the New Testament. However, we heard the saying, "what goes around comes around," so I think it's easy to presume that Paul inflicted the same torture he underwent after his conversion. I'm not trying to down my brother Paul; however, if we can check off our list not leaving someone for dead, murder, and denouncing all Christian beliefs, then I think we can assuredly say we are currently in better standing than him.

But maybe you're not. Perhaps you were an atheist, a convicted murderer facing death row: a low-life, grimy unfit human, unworthy of salvation. Paul still said that you are God's righteousness as long as you have faith in Christ Jesus.

Examining Paul's bold statement, I see that we are made the righteousness of God through Jesus Christ. That's great. Jesus died on the cross, and now we are right with God. Again, it seems like an infallible concept when we didn't do anything to deserve our rightful place in him. Jesus died on the cross; of course, this makes him the righteousness of God. That unselfish act alone should qualify him. However, he was without sin; he was already blameless. So it begs the question, why risk his perfect life for imperfect beings when Jesus was already in good standing with God?

I think sometimes we forget all the benefits that were associated with Calvary. As Christians, we understand through Jesus's death that our sins are forgiven, the wounds in his side heal us, and redemption with the Father is restored. Yet, when Jesus died, we also became the righteousness of God with significant benefits.

The Bible is filled with promises given to the children of God. However, I found that Proverbs 10 explicitly outlines the advantages of the righteous: provisions, blessings, and wealth. As I unpacked this chapter, I discovered that our righteousness frees us from death (verse 2). Now, of course, the majority of us will die. Our natural bodies are not immortal, as I am experiencing old age pains at this very instance. Yet, the death of Jesus means that we do not have to die a second death because his righteousness makes us blameless.

That's a clear spiritual blessing; however, God also provides for our natural needs as the righteous will never go hungry (verse 3). With the pandemic, toilet paper was not the only thing scarce. So was food. Nevertheless, I still gained fifteen pounds. It wasn't Joseph's seven-year famine but still a food shortage. Unfortunately, this is only the beginning, as the Bible warns of these things, but one thing is for sure; there will be manna for the righteous.

Another blessing is that the righteous will be remembered (verse 7). Our lives are recorded in the Lamb's book of life, yet the righteous are placed now. How many times have you heard stories of past saints who have gone to glory, but their memory remains? It is because God will not let the righteous be forgotten. We will never forget how they paved the way for us. Their earnest prayers had great power and produced wonderous results (Jas 5:16 NLT). Hence, we shall always be remembered because we are never removed from his sight (Prov 10:30).

Even after death, God still blesses his righteousness. However, he continuously blesses us in life. The power of life and death is in our tongues; therefore, our words have influence. Proverbs 10:11 states that the mouth of the righteous is a fountain of life and our tongue is choice silver (verse 20), which means there is power in our words, wisdom in our speech (verse 31), and victory in our praise. Thus when the righteous are closed-mouthed, we hold back the God-given power in our tongues. Since we are the righteousness of God, we can speak blessings over our lives because that's another benefit of Calvary.

One of the main benefits was that Jesus died, so we didn't have to. He delivered us from a deserved death (Prov 10:2). Remember, Jesus was faultless. He never sinned; however, he was made into a curse bearing the weight of sin for us. Jesus didn't deserve to die. Yet, we did. Considering our past wrongdoings, we should have been the ones bearing the stigma of the cross. It was our flesh that should have been pricked. Our hands and feet should have been stabbed with nails. A stake should have been thrust into our sides.

I AM THE RIGHTEOUSNESS OF GOD.

We deserved a horrific death but were somehow rewarded with everlasting life.

HE TOOK OUR PLACE AT CALVARY.

Even as a minister of the gospel, I am not without fault. I strive to live a holy life. However, sometimes my holiness seems questionable. I say wrong things, think evil, and fall victim to my flesh. I am an imperfect person whom God has called to preach to other flawed individuals.

Let's not get on your high horse, as you aren't perfect either. The only difference between you and me is that I'm just brave enough to write it. Therefore, when we look at all of our failings and how wrong we were, how can God still make that claim that we are his righteousness?

Jesus did not only take our place, but he traded places with us. We deserved death, so he died. We were sinful, so he became sin. We had no relationship with God, so he became the forsaken Son on our behalf. We were unrighteous, so he bore our sins for us to become the righteousness of God.

Jesus took a crown of thorns and gave us a crown of blessings (Prov 10:6). How remarkable is it that we are undeserving, but God continues to bless his people? His benefits go beyond job promotions, stock increases, and mega-million lottery wins. Those things are volatile and can fade with the wind. However, the provisions of God are everlasting. We are crowned with blessings of prosperity, health, and, most of all, eternal life.

We are joint-heirs with Christ in every aspect of the Kingdom. Jesus died once, so we would never have to die again. That is our divine inheritance as the children of God. Sure, we quickly remember that benefit and the spiritual materialisms of our mansions in the sky. However, can't we realize that we are also God's righteousness?

I know it is hard to fathom. However, we are in good standing with God regardless of our past sins. Now, I have done some dirt in my life. Remember, I was born in the church and had the title of a "church girl," which meant I had to prove that I wasn't. I did everything I could to separate myself from that embarrassing title. Yet, despite all my unrighteousness, I became alright with him once I gave up and surrendered my will to God.

My first experience in understanding that I was God's righteousness came when I was the president of my church organization's youth convention. I was probably the least qualified of the candidates, but somehow those people selected me to lead. Years ago, I previously was the vice president and did absolutely nothing in my title. Therefore, this time, I decided I would give God my all. I worked tirelessly to ensure that God would be satisfied with the convention. The weekend was almost over, and as I took inventory of my deeds, I asked God for confirmation.
"Did I do everything that you asked me to do?"
And God answered, "I am well-pleased."

I smiled, not understanding the significance until that Sunday. The Holy Spirit confirmed what God had said to me less than 24 hours ago. I jumped clear out of my seat, loudly crying out God's sentiments. Of course, the ride home was quite interesting as both parents laughed hysterically at my overly-enthusiastic praise. The banter at my expense quickly stopped when I asked if they ever heard God say he was well-pleased with anything they have done in their lives. The car was silent, and to add salt to their wounded spirit, I said, "Keep living holy, and maybe one day God will say he is well pleased with you."

Checkmate. I won that battle, but the real struggle was that of my mind. With all my past sins, God said he was satisfied with me. I could have died that moment and gone to Heaven. Years later, when sin entered my life again, I would wonder why he didn't just take me then. However, God said the exact words to me as he said to Jesus: "I am well pleased."

I honestly thought that those words were reserved for his perfect Begotten Son. Especially not the likes of me. There was no way that God, the Creator of all the World, would find delight in anything that I could do. After all, I was a confessed sinner, then a saint, a backslider back to a believer, redeemed but uncertain. My

I AM THE RIGHTEOUSNESS OF GOD.

journey of Christianity was a high-velocity roller coaster without the security of a seatbelt. Dangerously fatal, yet at that moment, God was pleased with me.

Again, this is very hard to believe. When God said those words to his Son, Jesus was recently baptized. For us, baptism symbolizes transforming from a sinful life to a life of holiness without sin. Jesus was faultless. He never sinned. So why would a perfect man need to be baptized? That was John the Baptist's question as well; nevertheless, Jesus was baptized that all righteousness would be fulfilled (Matt 3:15). In other words, Jesus' baptism was the start of his path to Calvary to make things right between God and his Creation.

Remember, this was the first event to propel Jesus's ministry. Jesus was known as the Bible speaks of his birth and being a child in the temple. Nevertheless, no miracles were recorded until after Jesus was baptized. When God said that he was well-pleased with Jesus, he knew that this was the start of his journey to redeem God's children back to him.

However, I did nothing of the sort. All I did was organize a measly youth event. As I recall, no one accepted Christ. No one decided to trade their filthy garments for salvation. It was a good convention, but nothing comparable to Jesus starting his ministry in my eyes. Yet, God was delighted with me.

Being God's righteousness has nothing to do with our good works. I'll admit that I worked relentlessly to ensure that God would be satisfied with the event throughout that year. Yet, my works did not put me in good standing with God. If it was not by works, then what was it?

As Christians, we often limit the righteousness of God to ethical standards. We strive to do what is correct through charitable donations, volunteering, and being a good person. However, no amount of volunteering nor generous contributions will buy our righteousness.

WE CAN'T BUY WHAT HAS ALREADY BEEN PURCHASED.

Jesus brought our righteousness with his Blood and called us to do good works. Nevertheless, being good stewards are the characteristics of being righteous; yet it has little to do with obtaining the title of the righteousness of God.

We can't earn our righteousness as it was given through acceptance and faith in Jesus Christ. Unbelievably, many people think. *"I am a good person; therefore, I am going to Heaven."* This statement is one of the biggest misconceptions that is a straight path to damnation. Do not pass Go, and no need for two hundred dollars. Charitable acts cannot accomplish what occurred at Calvary. Unfortunately, people honestly believe that their good deeds equate to what Jesus achieved on the cross.

We could work for a lifetime and never be able to pay God for the title of being his righteousness. Even Isaiah counted our righteous deeds like filthy rags (Isa 64:6). We are called to do good works (Eph 2:9 – 10), yet our efforts do not make us the righteousness of God. Only by faith in Jesus Christ can we be pleasing in the sight of God.

We cannot mistake self-righteousness for Godly righteousness. Self-righteous people focus on what they achieved versus giving God glory for what he allowed them to accomplish. Their boasting does not glorify God but screams, look at what I have done instead of placing the attention on him. When God said he was well-pleased with me, it had nothing to do with my good works but everything to do with my self-denial. That weekend was my total commitment to God, just as Jesus's baptism was his symbolic obligation to fulfill God's will.

I know that everything in us wants to resist the fact that we are the righteousness of God. Mainly because we know we aren't good enough. Even with all the things I accomplished during the youth event, I could have done much more. Nevertheless, God was pleased with what I did only because my heart desired to satisfy him above everything, and I still didn't feel righteous.

I AM THE RIGHTEOUSNESS OF GOD.

We don't deserve to be called his righteousness, but we cannot deny it. Denying this newfound label means that we ultimately spit on the cross. That isn't easy to digest as it was hard for me to write. Nonetheless, it's true. When we disallow ourselves to believe that we are God's righteousness, we reject the perfect gift of the cross, instinctively saying that his death was not good enough.

Refusing being his righteousness means that we call God a liar. I know it's difficult to admit, but that's what we unintentionally say when we deny our righteous identity. We make the cross an insignificant gesture because we merely do not believe in who God says we are.

When we became the righteousness of God, it was for our sake and his. God could have allowed us to be lost, having no relationship with him. Yet, he wanted the same connection with Adam to be restored within us. Therefore, God's divine love permitted the death of his Son, Jesus Christ, to remove us far from sin but distinctively closer to him.

I can't help but think that Jesus is enough. Jesus is perfect; God didn't need us. Who are we in comparison to his Son? God didn't have to restore his relationship with humanity. He could have easily destroyed the Earth during Sodom and Gomorrah. God could have demolished it with the flood. Even now, he could kill us all with Covid-19. We were not necessary. After all, he has the most extraordinary relationship with his divine Son, Jesus Christ, who is wholly and utterly perfect. Yet, God desired more, and that more was you and I.

Jesus is enough, but God chose to have a relationship with you. He didn't just desire you but placed you in good standing in him. Oddly enough, when Jesus died, you became joint-heirs with him, causing you to have the same righteousness that Jesus possesses. That's hard to recognize that you are just as righteous as Jesus Christ, a man who knew no sin but was made sin to acquire our righteousness. Again, it's another hard thing to type into this book. However, the death of Jesus means that we gain every benefit that God has granted him, which means that we are equally righteous and faultless, just as Christ.

This is a complex concept to understand, yet our lives will change if we wholeheartedly accept that we are God's righteousness. It is impossible to have faith in our salvation if we do not have confidence that we are morally just through the death of Jesus Christ (Rom 1:1). When Jesus died, we became the righteousness of God because our past, present, and future sins are and will be forgiven. Meaning that as long as we can repent, the all-knowing God will cause himself to have amnesia, forgetting our prior transgressions. He will not remember our sinful state but look at us as he looks at Jesus, full of righteousness.

That's the power of the cross. That the omniscient God, who knows everything, will fail to remember your transgressions because of one sacrificial death. You remember your sins. Your friends and family won't let you forget them, but somehow God only sees the Blood. He only finds his virtue instead of evil, goodness versus corruption. You are in good standing with God. Wouldn't it be great if people could see you as God sees you? It would be even more remarkable if you could see yourself in that image, full of God's righteousness.

Chapter 4

I am the temple of God.

"Know ye not that ye are the temple of God, and that the Spirit of God dwelleth in you?"

—1 Corinthians 3:16

I don't do windows.

Nor do I reline shelves, move furniture, clean dust bunnies, remove cobwebs or reorganize kitchen cabinets. Occasionally, I forget to throw away expired condiments and remove food from my pantry. I rarely unclog my drains. I dare not disturb the sanctity of a bug's final resting place. I let them rest in peace.

Monsters aren't under my bed, just piles of dust. Ten years in my home, and I've never washed my curtains or had my area rug professionally cleaned. Febreeze will do. I don't dust my vents or my walls frequently. I totally avoid window sills, cleaning dryer ducts, coils, and gutters. Oh yeah, and most importantly, I don't do windows.

I don't particularly like cleaning. Never have, and probably never will. Yet, I will get on my hands and knees to scrub a floor in a seldomly visited space in my church. I will dry mop unreachable walls, clean behind heavy pulpit chairs, dust every decorative flower, and wipe down every pew and seat in the sanctuary. I will even go as far as to sanitize urinals, and on occasions, I have been known to clean the entire church by myself. Ironically, only at my church will I do windows.

Again, I do not like cleaning. So, why do it?

Simply because it is God's house and his presence is there. I haven't cleaned the church often because, well, did I mention, I don't particularly enjoy cleaning. However, I take pleasure in humbling myself to tidy God's house. I will vacuum the sanctuary, polish the pulpit, and dust the organ keys. I will do what is necessary as I enjoy becoming a maid for the King.

I clean my church thoroughly, but, in truth, the church is just a building. Sure, God's presence is there. However, it is only a four-wall structure, a building where we gather to worship. Of course, no one wants to enter a filthy sanctuary with fingerprints on the glass, water bottles under the pews, and trash on the floor. We want our churches to look spotless, fit for worship, and a place for God to reside. However, Paul said, God's actual dwelling place is inside us.

Now, I *really* don't like cleaning, but it's necessary.

When he told this to the church of Corinth, I am sure he got some peculiar looks. After all, it's outlandish to think that God resides within our physical bodies. Even hearing sermons and statements that we are God's temple still makes me feel a little perplexed. When I consider my body, I have to think, "why on Earth would the Almighty God want to dwell in this floppy, unsightly thing?"

Paul would have called me a carnal-minded Christian, stating that I lacked the spiritual maturity to understand that I am indeed God's sanctuary. I would have said, "you are absolutely right." The idea that God lives inside me always causes me to look down and examine my physical state. Then I laugh, remembering a Golden Girls' episode where Sophia pretends to be possessed by Rose's dead husband. When Rose reveals that Charlie used her body, Sophia says, "if I knew he was coming, I would have tidied up a bit." That's exactly how I feel when I consider that I am God's temple.

I AM THE TEMPLE OF GOD.

How is it that the Almighty God, who has created the magnificence of Heaven, the splendor of this Earth, wants to dwell in an overweight saggy vessel? Why would God want to live in me when he could ultimately live anywhere in the universe? Considering the numerous fat cells and the food I put in my body, I can't fathom why he would choose to dwell in me. It almost makes me want to change my diet. Well, almost.

Ironically, I am the perfect residence for God, and so are you. No matter how many pounds I gain or how many pastries I consume, God still wants to reside in me. Incredibly, God loves us that much to humble himself to dwell with us every second of the day, confining himself to a body that many want to change.

We tend to see ourselves as unsuitable and unattractive as we would like to improve our physical state. Even now, I have been desperately attempting to remove my fupa. I've tried every exercise to eliminate the fat. However, that does not matter to God. We could attempt to lose a few pounds, but God does not consider whether we are a size 2 or 42. When God looks for a dwelling place, he looks for a clean vessel, a body willing to be used for his glory. So, don't worry if you aren't a supermodel's size. God sees you as prime real estate as long as you have a renewed mind and a clean heart.

Our thoughts must be converted to believe that we are God's temple. We often confess to having the indwelling of the Holy Spirit but forget that we are God's temple. So what does that mean?

Considering the Holy Trinity, there is God, the Father, the Son, and the Spirit. If we pondered the question, where does the Godhead live? Many of us will state that God lives in Heaven with his Son, Jesus Christ, who is sitting on the right side of his Father. If we asked the same question concerning the Holy Ghost, the answer would be inside you and me.

GOD'S SPIRIT SHOULD NOT BE HOMELESS.

When God formed Adam, he breathed his breath or spirit in him, causing Adam to live. The Holy Spirit is a life-giving agent that brought forth life, and thousands of years later, every human and every creature is using the same breath of God. Remarkably, everything that has breath has a small measure of God's Spirit dwelling inside them to live. God made us in his image, and since God is a spirit, he provided his spirit inside of us all. Without it, death occurs as no one can survive without breathing.

Nevertheless, the Spirit of God created natural life for all and spiritual life for others. God chooses to live inside of those who have a clean vessel. Our insides might be plagued with high cholesterol, poor glucose levels, and unhealthy toxins that cause us to whither away daily. Yet, when God chooses a dwelling place, he does not consider our physical state but our spiritual health. We are afflicted with unsightly physical bodies, yet God only concerns himself with the well-being of our spirit. He seeks a clean residence that has ridden itself from sinful debris, spiritually cleaned for his dwelling, ready to be used for his purpose.

GOD CANNOT DWELL IN AN UNCLEAN VESSEL.

Again, let me remind you I don't particularly appreciate cleaning or getting repairs done. Never have and probably never will. However, spiritually, I have to clean myself daily, sometimes hourly. I have to admit. I am not a perfect residence. I sometimes have a few wall cracks that need patching, a few floorboards that need to be replaced, and occasionally I experience power outages. However, I must continuously keep my inner home in proper working condition as my landlord is constantly there.

Jesus is our landlord. I know my mother is probably laughing at this statement as there was a song that we despised that said, "Jesus, you're my landlord, and there is a leak in this old building." The words are, well, relevant. Nevertheless, it reminded us of some backwood country bumkins singing in floppy hats and swaying church fans from side to side. Yet, the truth is that the Godhead is our landlord, our handyman, and our tenant. He understands that our buildings aren't perfect; that's why God provided the Holy Spirit to fix the leaks in our facilities.

I AM THE TEMPLE OF GOD.

As a child of God, we undergo home inspection to ensure that our bodies are a living sacrifice, holy and acceptable for his use (Rom 12:1). I know that it seems as if we must be continuously perfect. Again, I am not without flaws. I have never been and probably never will be. Yet we must do all we can to ensure that our bodies are satisfactory for his living.

Think of our bodies as our natural homes. We clean our homes consistently, ensuring they are neat and suitable for living. Yet, we may sometimes leave dishes in the sink, clothes miss the hamper, and our floors may need good vacuuming. We don't place our homes on the market because they need cleaning. We don't sell them because they are untidy. Instead, we start sprucing up a bit.

Being the temple of God means we constantly clean his dwelling place like we clean our homes through repentance. Unfortunately, no matter how vigorously we clean, there is always dirt behind the fridge, dust bunnies under the sofa, and cobwebs in the corner. We may never get it spotless no matter how much Mr. Clean or Pinesol we use. Yet, we still try until our houses smell like a chemical lab explosion.

Just like our homes will never be spotless, God knows we will not be perfect. He understands that we will miss the mark and come short of his glory by saying and doing the wrong things. Thankfully, he provided the best cleaning agent, the Blood of Jesus Christ, for those hard-to-get-out stains.

The Blood is the only cleaning solution for our spiritual homes. I have done a lot of dirt in my life. So much grime that I thought it was impossible ever to be clean. My sins were significant blemishes in my life. However, when the Blood of Jesus was applied, my sinful stains were lifted miraculously.

I know this sounds like an infra commercial in which you are waiting to hear: *"Are you having trouble with fornication? Tried everything and can't get rid of pride? You've tried all your life, but you can't stop lying? We have the solution to those hard-to-remove sins, The Blood of Jesus Christ. Act now, and you can have the best cleaning agent, The Blood, for four easy payments of $39.99. But wait, if you call now, you can have this leading cleaning solution for three* *easy payments of $29.99"*. However, this is no infra commercial. There are no payments. Thankfully, the Blood of Jesus Christ has been paid in full. Ask now, and you can have it for free.

That's the power of The Blood. God knows that his temple will need cleaning. Yet, he did not leave us without a proper cleaning solution. He has provided his Son's blood that wipes away every sin imaginable. Our temples are kept clean through The Blood.

Wouldn't it be great to have a cleaner like this for our homes? If you look under my sink, you will find several bottles for sanitizing, cleaning, disinfecting, washing, scrubbing, polishing, etc. Again, I don't like cleaning, but it's necessary, especially when I have a guest coming. I will clean my home vigorously to ensure that I'm not talked about because I don't particularly enjoy cleaning. However, do we do that for God?

I can't help imagining what Zacchaeus thought when Jesus said he wanted to visit his home. There were no cell phones, so Zacchaeus couldn't go on IG to send a DM to bae saying, "BTW, Jesus is coming… IRL, RN, HMU!" The best he could do was hope that his wife didn't leave any fraudulent tax papers on the table. I'm confident the following text would have been, "Burn everything!"

Could you imagine the amount of cleaning we would do if God said he would physically visit our houses? Undoubtedly, we would tidy our homes for days, if not weeks. We would surely clean those hard-to-reach areas that are often neglected—moving sturdy furniture, wiping down every wall, sweeping under the rug. After all, he would know if we didn't. Ironically, God constantly dwells inside us, knowing our laziness in spiritual tidiness. Therefore, we should self-examine ourselves regularly, ensuring that our temple is always clean for God's use.

God wants to live in us, and we should welcome the notion that he does. If we could fathom what that means for a moment, I believe we would be delivered from fear and doubt. Fear is the destroyer of faith. However, if God is our light and our salvation, if he is the strength of our lives, then why are we afraid? Our faith in God should diminish all of life's fears. We have the most powerful being living on the inside, so why should we be afraid?

I am the Temple of God.

Having God dwelling inwardly means he protects, defends, counsels, teaches, and supports us twenty-four hours a day. We have a constant bodyguard always willing to fight on our behalf, which should increase our assurance and weaken fear.

When his enemies came to eat his flesh, David said they stumbled and fell (Ps 27:2). David was human and undoubtedly felt the same anxiety we feel when met with life challenges. However, even as a great warrior, David did not trust his sword but in the Lord.

David did not have the Holy Spirit inside him as it only came upon him (1 Sam 16:13). Yet, God was still there. Since we are now the temple of God, and the Spirit lives in us, how much more will God lift a standard to protect us against every obstacle and challenge that comes our way?

Remarkably, God wants to dwell with us every waking moment of our lives. Many people initially believed God visited Adam and Eve in the Garden of Eden. However, I think God did not only visit them, but he dwelled among them. God had a close relationship with Adam. He walked and talked with him, allowing Adam to name all the animals, giving him complete dominion over the land. Therefore, it is safe to presume that God's appearance did not only happen once Adam and Eve sinned, but he was always there (Gen 3:8).

Consider how God must have loved Adam and Eve as they were his finest creation. They were the first of many. It's uncanny to think that God would have created them in the Garden and then returned to Heaven. Without saying, it would seem reasonable that God humbled himself to live among his first human children. Therefore, it is more realistic to believe that God left his throne to dwell among them in Paradise.

When God finished making man, he saw that it was excellent, indicating that Adam and Eve were his best workmanship. They were perfect and had an honest relationship with God because it was not disrupted by sin or corrupted by distractions. God knew this relationship would end once sin snaked itself into the world. Therefore, God would not have left Adam and Eve alone in Eden.

He would have relished in the moment of having a lucid connection with them as He would foreseeably never have a flawless fellowship with humanity after sin ever again.

Ironically, this would not be the first time God humbled himself to live with his children. God gave Moses clear instructions on constructing the temple and the ark of the covenant as God wanted to dwell, meet, and commune with the Israelites (Ex 25:8, 22). Now consider this: "The Earth is the Lord's, and the fulness thereof," right? Then why would the great big wonderful God want to reside in a tent, let alone a box?

Think about it. A God not constrained by time, place, or space confined himself to a 52x31x31 inch bin. God could have lived anywhere. Yet, he bound his splendor to be placed on top of a portable container. No bigger than a dog's crate to be closer to his people.

God, the Father, and God, the Son, are eternal, meaning they live forever. However, Jesus Christ, who could not die, surrendered himself to death so we might have the indwelling of God's spirit. He did not have to taste the bitterness of death. Nevertheless, he humbled himself to the cross. He became bound by sin, made into a curse to ensure that we have the benefits of the Holy Ghost. Jesus Christ did the unthinkable; he died so he could make us God's dwelling place.

We may not be ornamented in gold molding and made of gold like the ark of the covenant. Yet, we should consider that human hands made the ark. We, on the other hand, were fashioned by God. God designed and created us for this very purpose. He made reservations two thousand years ago to ensure we had a vacancy for him. Therefore, we should not think that we are unworthy to be his temple. Instead, we should consider how valuable we are to God.

As the temple of God, you are his last earthly resting place. You are where he chooses to be. God could reside anywhere within the universe, yet he selected you and me. It's incredible to think that God loves us that much to constrain himself to us daily. We are intolerable and undeserving, yet he takes up residence, cleaning out our hearts while filling us with his divine love.

When Isaiah proclaimed that Emmanuel would be with you, he spoke not metaphorically but literally. God was in the Garden with Adam and Eve as he was in the tabernacle, the ark of the covenant, and Solomon's temple. In the new testament, God walked among them in the flesh as Jesus Christ, and when he ascended to Heaven, the Spirit of God descended into you and me. Your body is his final residence until Christ returns to bring you home. You are the temple of God, a perfect living place. God chose you as he never wants to be too far away. He lives inside you to defend, protect, and guide you through life's challenges. Never fear, as the Almighty God has chosen the most prime viable residence inside you.

Now, I don't particularly like cleaning. Never have and probably never will. However, I am glad I don't have to clean by myself. Thankfully, the Almighty God is an excellent tenant who wipes away all the hard-to-remove sinful stains from my heart. He cleans the hard-to-reach places of my mind, the evil thoughts hidden away that I didn't even think were there. He rids me of the waste of fear and doubt and replenishes me with the fragrance of his divine love. Most of all, I don't do windows. Yet, he cleans the windows of my soul to see the best of me.

Chapter 5

I am God's workmanship.

"For we are his workmanship, created in Christ Jesus unto good works, which God hath before ordained that we should walk in them."

—EPHESIANS 2:10

IF GIVEN A CHOICE, would you rather have a Ford Focus or a Bugatti Veyron? Like me, you probably never heard of a Bugatti, a Pagani, or a Mazzanti. Or any foreign car that is hard to pronounce ending in the letter I. However, given the name, I would definitely go with the Bugatti. Anything that ends in a vowel just sounds more expensive, right?

The Ford and the Bugatti have the same ratings for durability and stability. They equally are two reliable vehicles, with one slight difference. A fully-loaded Ford Focus currently costs around $25,000, while a standard Bugatti would rate at one hundred times that amount. That's right, an astounding 2.5 million dollars. If you want to get from point A to B, you may pick the Ford. However, if you want to arrive at your destination in style, you are going with the Bugatti.

At first glance, the Bugatti seems more desirable because of its slick design, magnificent exterior, and futuristic structure. This car looks like something that should be featured in a Sci-Fi movie. I'm not a car buff, but I am sure this car can fly. Okay, well, maybe it can't take flight. However, I bet it could talk. If Knight Rider could talk decades ago, surely this car should speak at least six different languages.

Then let's look at the Ford Focus. It's a good vehicle with the same quality rating as the Bugatti, but it's an everyday car. Nothing fancy about it, just an infotainment system that provides a wireless mobile connection. Again, it's a nice feature, but it doesn't compare to the Bugatti's capabilities, and I'm positively sure the Ford Focus can't fly.

The Ford also is comparably similar to other cars on the road. In fact, I am pretty sure that the Nissan Sentra is a distant cousin. However, the Bugatti doesn't have any counterparts that compare. Sure, there's the Koenigsegg CCXR or the Hennessey Venom GT. Yet, I think we wouldn't mistake those cars for any Ford. The structures of all those cars alone make them more desirable than the dime-a-dozen Ford Focus. Trust me; if we were ever blessed to see a Veyron firsthand, we would break our necks to take notice.

It's all about the quality of the two vehicles. Even though they both have the same rating, the creation of the two makes them significantly different. The Bugatti takes six months to manufacture, while the Ford assembly line can produce a Focus within less than two days. The reason is that the high-performing French car manufacturers assemble each of its 1,800 parts by hand, ensuring that this vehicle's craftsmanship is second to none. Consequentially, ensuring that this car would be worth 100 times more than the equally rated Ford Focus.

At this point, I am positive you are thinking, "so what?" You probably don't care about cars, especially since you can't afford a Veyron and possibly have a Ford Focus parked in your driveway. However, the idea is that two objects, like automobiles, can have the same rating quality and can have the same capabilities. Still, one's worth appears more extraordinary because of its craftsmanship.

You are the extraordinary, as you are the Bugatti.

Again, I am sure you wonder how you are the Bugatti when you feel more like the Ford. As I said, the Ford Focus is an everyday car. It's a suitable vehicle, nothing fancy, just a regular blue-collar car. On the other hand, the Bugatti is exceptional. It's one of the most exquisite vehicles on the market, and I am pretty sure it can fly.

However, you can't fly.

Your net worth may never reach the cost of a Veyron, and there is nothing slick or magnificent about your exterior. It may look like a dented-aged lemon reaching two hundred thousand miles on a dead battery with lots of junk in the trunk. Even though you may see yourself as the Ford, as there is nothing remarkable about you, God sees you as the Bugatti. After all, you are his most incredible creation.

In Genesis, God created the entire world and everything within it in six days. God said, "let there be light," and the light occurred. God spoke at the beginning of creation, and everything appeared in existence. Yet, when God formed Adam, he did the extraordinary. He constructed Adam out of the dust, forming and molding man by his mighty hand. God's *voice* created the world, but his *hands* produced man.

Let's think about that for a moment. We often get excited about God speaking the stars and the moon into existence. Yet, we rarely get excited that the Almighty God took the time to create his divine workmanship. He took time to construct Adam and Eve. God did not just speak them into reality. However, I believe God came down from Heaven to make, shape, and mold them into what he wanted them to be.

That's how valuable we are to God. If we could just ponder how massive our world is, we may think that we are pretty insignificant with all the galaxies, stars, and planets. Nevertheless, God only spoke those things into existence. He just said it, and it happened. We may seem trivial when we consider the universe and everything in it, but we must understand that we are the perfect workmanship of God. Despite the massiveness and splendor of this universe, we cannot forget that we are more remarkable as God produced us by hand, breathing his divine spirit in humanity. We are the Bugattis and not the Fords.

We are valuable in the sight of God because we are his workmanship. God made the splendor of this world, and the most magnificent creation was you, and I. God loved us so much that he made us in his image. He constructed us out of nothing and made us into something of worth. Who could do that but God? The best thing I can make out of dust is a mud pie. However, God made his finest creation out of Earth, causing us to be something of value and worth.

God knows our worth, and he will protect his investment. If, by some miracle, someone gave us a Bugatti, we wouldn't park this car in our driveways to tempt thieves or vandals with the opportunity to destroy its structure. We would undoubtedly keep this car in the garage and safe from the elements. After all, it is a 2.5 million dollar car.

If we would do that much for the Bugatti, how much more do you think God would do to protect our value? God shields, watches, and clothes his best creation. He will not allow the thief to come "steal, kill, and destroy" his most prized possession. Instead, God conserves us under his wings, ensuring that we keep our worth to do good works.

When Ettore Arco Isidoro Bugatti manufactured the Veyron, he did not believe its purpose was to be a simple showpiece. Nor did he create it ineffectually. Yet, he designed this car to be one of the fastest, most luxurious vehicles globally. Therefore, God did not fashion us as useless pieces of art. He did not intend for us to sit dormant on the shelf. However, he designed us with purpose.

God has endowed in you a special gift to be used to build his Kingdom. When we think of our abilities, we often discount them as mere talents when they were God-produced. This is the same God who created the mountains, the canyons, and the waterfalls. He made all of this, and do you genuinely think he would then be slack with his finest workmanship? Of course not.

I'm no car manufacturer; however, I believe that every car manufacturer has a particular purpose for their inventions. Some cars are more durable; they can take a beating. Other cars are more reliable, while some vehicles are built for speed. Some vehicles are equipped to carry heavy loads, while some are made small for the environment. Each company gave each one of its cars a purpose to fulfill.

God created us all the same but different. He has given us unique gifts and talents to be used to build his Kingdom. Some God gave the ability to sing, while others he gave the power to minister. Some of his Creations are good at figures, while the others are good at spending them. I believe every human has a talent or a gift that God manufactured in them before the beginning. However, it is up to us to put the key in the ignition.

Years ago, I taught a family resiliency course. The class offered case studies where the students must determine the person's strengths. One scenario involved a prostitute whose abusive drug-dealing boyfriend murdered her three-year-old son. My students could often detect the case study character's strengths; however, this scenario always confused them.

After a few minutes of pondering, they realized that the prostitute had used her resources to provide her child with food and shelter. Following much discussion, many realized that she was probably stronger than most. She survived in the direst situations because she used what she had. It wasn't her body that she used, but her survival instinct. We may not always recognize our abilities, but they are there, ready to be used. We cannot allow ourselves to be perplexed in our purpose.

Just think what that prostitute could have done for the Kingdom of God. She could have used her talents to help in the woman or homeless ministry. She could have easily taught others who were financially unstable how to survive. Even after her experiences as a prostitute, she could have started a grief group in her church or helped other young girls realize their worth. She could have effortlessly become a missionary because she was a people person and fearless. Don't discount the people in the streets; those individuals could become the greatest evangelist.

What would happen if those sinners we tend to overlook utilized their God-given talents for the Kingdom of God? Drug dealers are natural businessmen; gamblers know how to take risks. Drug addicts could become the best deacons as most are natural-born handymen, fixing anything to get their fix. The point is that God has given everyone gifts and talents that should be used for the Kingdom, yet most misuse them.

Now, let's not get upset with the drug dealer or the prostitute who is not using their gifts for God when we allow ours to sit docile. At least they are using theirs, just for the wrong team. However, we are on the winning side and still afraid to use what God gave us because we are unwilling to believe we can do what God has called us to do.

Unfortunately, many Christians tend to measure their gifts against other Christians. If they do it better, then why should we even try? The truth is that we cannot allow people to hinder our God-given assignments. We must focus on what God has assigned to our hands and perform it to the best of our abilities. God does not require perfection, but he does demand obedience.

I am not a perfect preacher; I am barely an ideal human. So, when God called me into the ministry, I did not answer the call. I put him directly on mute mode, screened his call like I do everyone in my life, and he, unlike my family, *actually* wanted something. I wasn't trying to be complicated. I wasn't trying to be disobedient; I was trying to be perfect.

I knew God had called me into ministry, but I was ill-equipped. I felt I never would measure up to those men and women who could make their voices rise and fall with the music. In my eyes, that was perfection, and I am a background singer. I'm definitely not in front. Most times, I have to rely on my cousin to give me my note. So there was no way I could add a few rolled chords or vibratos to my sermons. I couldn't even tell my godbrother what key I was in; hilariously, he doesn't even play when I preach. Even my father tried to teach me how to do this once, but I wouldn't even try. I was just me. There was no way I could stir the hearts of men by my voice alone. Ironically, when I did speak, everyone was silent.

There were no amens. No, "thank you, Jesus." No one bellowed out, "you better preach" or "take your time." So, I would typically speed up because it was dead silence. It was always dead silence. That's why I knew I was better off being a laity speaker than an actual preacher.

However, one Sunday, one of the ministers told me, "When people are quiet, they listen." She said, "Be careful when they are answering too much because it's here today but gone tomorrow." I understood, even though I would like an amen or some music now and then. However, I understood what she was saying. God had given me a different method of preaching that led people to listen.

Over the years, I began to worry less about others. I started developing what God had given to me and what God gave me was the gift of teaching. Teachers are pretty different than preachers. Preachers state what God requires. On the other hand, teachers explain how to achieve it. That's who I was. I was there to fill in the gaps. I was there to answer the questions that were left on the table. Once I realized that my gift was equally important, I began to feel more confident in who I am in God.

I understood that I could only be who God designed me to be. Even with all the billions of people in the world, there is still only one me and only one you. There is no point in trying to imitate people that can never be duplicated.

God, like the Ford, mass-produced man, but in his divine wisdom, somehow, he created each of us exceptionally like the Bugatti. No doubt, there are people in this world that look like us, act, walk and maybe even talk like us. However, we aren't that easily replicated. God made each of us unique and different in our particular way for his identified intent.

Understanding what God has placed inside you will help you achieve your purpose primarily because God has equipped you with the knowledge and the ability to do so. This first begins with trusting in God. We must trust our manufacturer. As I said before, you must put the key in the ignition, believing that God will start moving in your life.

We don't know what God has in store through your gifts. However, I know that whatever is inside of you is perfectly designed to be used by you for the glory of God. No great person knew the weight of their capabilities until they tried. Noah had to trust God to save his family. Joshua had to believe in him to save a nation, and Jesus trusted his Father to save the world. You have the gift of God; who knows what your abilities will accomplish until you trust him?

Yes, you will make mistakes, and you may fail. Yet, you cannot allow your gift to sit idle. By doing so, you have explicitly neglected God's plan for you. Trusting God means trusting his plan. The journey will not always be easy. However, you are the Bugatti, the "quest for perfection" built "Ford tough." God is your GPS, willing and ready to lead you to your destination, prepared to guide you through the task.

We must acknowledge that when God provides what seems to be an impossible mission, he has already given us the knowledge, skill, and wisdom to perform it. God will never give us a task to fulfill without first crafting the ability to complete his assignment. That wouldn't profit God. Why would he send you ill-equipped to fail? That's like a car manufacturer producing a car without an engine. They know it will not go far without it. Yet, they provide the necessary parts to ensure that the car's purpose will be achieved. God has designed us with the essential tools to accomplish our God-given assignments. We are equipped to do the task, and God is the gas that allows us to keep moving forward to arrive at victory.

Our victory is knowing that God did not create defective people. God designed us perfectly, even with our character and physical flaws. Those flaws have a purpose. Looking in the mirror, it's hard not to see all the imperfections that lay before us. Though, we are not poorly made. The workmanship of God is flawless. We may see ourselves as imperfect, but a perfect God made us just the way we are for his divine purpose.

WE ARE ALL UNIQUELY MADE

Think for a moment if Oprah Winfrey was trapped in Beyonce's body and vice versa. I know it's pretty hard to imagine, well, maybe not for Stedman. However, think about it. What would have been the outcome if God gave Oprah Beyonce's body while maintaining her sense of gab? Would Oprah still be known as the "Queen of All Media"? Or would people not have taken her as seriously? What if Beyonce had Oprah's features? Would there even be an anthem for single women? Probably not, because I doubt Ms. Sophia's knees could handle the choreography.

Let's think about one of my favorite celebrities, the Italian Stallion, Mr. Sylvester Stallone. What would have happened if his face was not paralyzed during birth, causing him to have his famous slurred speech? Would he still have been believable as a down-on-his-luck Philadelphia fighter with the eye of the tiger? Would his "Yo, Adrian" be as beloved if his voice sounded like James Earl Jones? Probably not, as my favorite movies would have never existed, nor would the spin-off movie Creed. And what would the world do if they could not see Michael B. Jordon topless? Seriously, because of that slurred speech, Michael B is topless! The fact is that people may see you as flawed, but the mere fact is that God made you impeccably perfect for whatever task that he intended.

WE AREN'T PERFECT, BUT WE ARE PERFECTLY MADE.

God ideally uses our imperfections to create a perfect plan for our lives. Even with our weaknesses, God can use them to accomplish greatness. We will never know what we are capable of unless we rid ourselves of discounting what God has manufactured inside, as he did not overlook any skill or ability. We only fail when we forget who made us. God is our creator who has equipped us with every spiritual gift needed to accomplish his great plan. Fortunately, those flaws we concern ourselves with were a part of that plan. We tend to think of our shortcomings as hindrances when they are merely aids to show the glory of God.

Our flaws make us the perfect workmanship of God to showcase his power and might. Who would thought a barren 90-year-old woman could produce an entire nation? Or how could a man with a limp walk upright before God? Is it possible for a blind man to see his healing or a depressed king to rule a country? Everyone has something that makes them seem ill-equipped for the job. Some bible scholars even think that Samson was autistic, which all signs seem to point that way, and look what he accomplished. The fact is that God will use what we feel is a weakness as our strength.

We are God's perfect workmanship, formed by the same God who created Heaven and Earth, the moon, the sun, and the stars. With all their brilliance, they still shine. They still stand with God, merely speaking them into existence. Yet, the almighty God shaped and formed you and me. Since this occurred, how much greater are we than those things he only spoke into reality?

God had his hands on us before the beginning of time, shaping and constructing us into his perfect image. Remember, we are the admirable workmanship of God. The picture-perfect design that he wants to showcase and use for his divine glory. Never forget that we have been created perfectly to do the good works of God as we are to achieve excellence. We are not defective, yet the best manufacturer has ideally designed us. We have been created by the hands of God to last. We aren't the Ford, but the Bugatti.

Chapter 6

I am fearfully and wonderfully made.

"I will praise thee; for I am fearfully and wonderfully made: marvellous are thy works; and that my soul knoweth right well."

—PSALMS 139:14

SINCE SHE WAS A little girl, my daughter wanted to be a doctor, particularly an OB/GYN. She would find health shows to watch nearly every day dealing with pain, blood, gore, or as she called it, labor and delivery. Most children wanted to watch cartoons, and she would like nothing more than to observe the horrors of childbirth intently. I thought she was a strange child, but I supported her career choices. After all, it was better than her first, a Barbie tattoo artist. Therefore, becoming a doctor was high on my list, especially if she became a plastic surgeon.

I tried everything to change her mind. She would have more manageable hours as babies are unpredictable and facelifts are conveniently scheduled. Her income would be substantially better, and most importantly, her dear mother could get free cosmetic surgery or at least weekly botox. Of course, she was dead set against it.

I AM FEARFULLY AND WONDERFULLY MADE.

Grabbing the excess bulge around my waist and unflattering gluteus-maximus, I continued to plead my case. To say the least, my little one was unmoved and even looked at me in disbelief when I asked about a family discount. At times, I would go so far as to show her pictures before she was born, accusing her of adding this unnecessary fat to my once slender frame. Again, my daughter was unmoved. As she was about to exit, I gave my last appeal saying everyone in the world is unhappy with their bodies. She laughed and said, "They can't be that unhappy because the world still needs OB/GYNs." Checkmate, she won.

Truthfully, even if my daughter obliged my absurd notion, I would still constantly focus on my body's imperfections. I have an entire list of things I would tuck, remove, lift, alter and change. My nose could be a tad smaller, my butt could benefit from a Brazilian Butt Lift, my waistline could be more defined, and my back fat connected to my front fat could be removed. Given the opportunity, I could probably design a perfect me, but I don't think I would still be satisfied.

Like me, I am sure if someone gave you a golden ticket to alter your appearance, you wouldn't hesitate for one second. Imagine the possibility of having muscular legs, thighs that can crush pineapples, breasts that barely move, and six-pack abs that could be used as a charcuterie board. The possibilities would be endless. It's unfortunate, but when we look in the mirror, we can fully account for everything we would change about our bodies because we don't recognize our value.

Throughout my teen years, that's how I felt compared to my friend Tasha. We both grew up together since preschool, and together, we blossomed into attractive girls. However, it seemed that someone watered and plucked her weeds more because she was a beautiful rose, and I felt more like a prickly cactus. Sure, I was pretty, but I had toothpicks for legs, bowling balls for breasts, and I was deadly afraid to smile during a thunderstorm. Saying I was awkwardly ill-portioned seems to be an understatement. So, I became her sidekick, the seemingly no-named girl, Tasha's friend.

This is how I felt for most of my high school career until we studied abroad in Mexico. After that, my life changed completely.

I had studied Spanish for three years and knew how to speak the most critical phrases fluently: mainly greetings, locating the bathroom, and how much this cost. However, when we entered customs, I started hearing words being shouted at me I had never heard. I kept looking down to ensure toilet paper wasn't stuck to the bottom of my feet or that I didn't have half the flight's meal in my teeth. None of these things occurred, so I was confused about why they only directed their attention toward me. So I did the only thing that came naturally, I graciously bowed, forgetting that I was in Mexico and not Japan, and smiled.

Thankfully, the men smiled back but repeated, "eres bella, eres bonita." I smiled and bowed again, trying to give any courtesy I could muster to hide my ignorance. They returned the same gesture, smiling and profusely nodding while repeating the unfamiliar words. We all looked like a bunch of bobble-headed grinning fools.

This was the end of the road for the small mob who followed me as I finally reached the customs agent. Yet, the smiling continued, but gratefully he spoke English. He returned my documents and inquired if I knew what the men were saying to me. I knew they weren't asking where the bathroom was and how much I cost, thankfully!

"The men say you are beautiful and pretty. And you are."
In disbelief, I pointed at Tasha, then the customs agent shook his head and said, "*no, eres tu,*" meaning "no, it's you." That day I added a few more words to my Spanish vocabulary.

Something amazing had occurred. Men around the globe ignored my beautiful friend and started noticing me. This was as foreign to me as the Mexican city I found myself in; however, I eagerly obliged the welcomed sentiments. Hilariously, I was an international beauty and hadn't realized it. I laughed at the idea, but one thing for sure, I could not deny that I was more desirable than I thought. Despite this newly established confidence, the moment only lasted for the length of my trip. Seven days.

I was back home without the compliments of Mexican men in airports, restaurants, or on the streets. There were no more Jamaican men fresh off the cruise ship or handsome Cuban and Colombians who asked me to dance. I was back home with the same country bumkins I grew up with since kindergarten, and none of them looked at me the way those men had. Sure, the guys in my town were nice to me in that "let's be friends" sort of way. However, none of them seemed to share the sentiments of all the men I encountered on my trip. The guys back home just thought I was funny.

And that was true. Mostly, I always had a loud, outgoing nature, complimented by a good sense of humor. If I weren't beautiful, I would be hysterical or, as my friends called it, 'crazy.' My shenanigans could always make people laugh. I loved my personality until, one day, the most handsome senior inquired about me as a freshman. I didn't even think he knew my name, but he did. As I intently eavesdropped on my cousin's conversation. I never will forget what he said.

"I thought about dating her; she is cute but too quirky."

Well, that was that. Not only did I have to worry about my body image, but I could also add my personality to the list. Apparently, some people thought my comedic behaviors were bizarre, weird, strange, and quirky. Quirky. The one word seemed like death by a thousand insults. Did people really see me as odd? Sure, I was a little eccentric, but quirky? Quirky was Screech Powers and not me. I was more like Lisa Turtle and Kelly Kapowski, wrapped into a neat five-foot-six container. Yet unknowing to me, people viewed me as, well, quirky.

I began to worry too much about what people thought. Between my negative views of my body and my personality, I became a shell of a person. Depression crept in by the time I was a freshman in college. One thing that college taught me was there was a world of "Tashas" on campus. These girls were glamorous, hailing from major metro cities, dressed in the latest fashions. I was a country girl with an accent from a rural town with only one clothing store. And there was no way I could compete, so I gave up.

I didn't feel like I could measure up to those girls, especially when I couldn't even measure up to my friends back home. Therefore I gave up, threw in the towel, waved the white flag. I couldn't keep up with their good looks, intelligence, or personality. I learned there was nothing special about me compared to everyone in my life.

It's unfortunate, but I compared myself to others my entire life. Maybe, this is something that I learned from my mother. She would constantly assess me against my childhood best friend, Sherrell. Sherrell, in my eyes, was perfect and, apparently, to my mother as well. Whenever I did something not up to my mother's standards, she would bellow, "Do you think Sherrell would do that?" Instead of thinking WWJD, "What would Jesus do?" it was more like WWSD. Finally, I got enough courage to tell my mother that I wasn't Sherrell; I was just me. My mother didn't realize it and apologized. However, the fact is that I didn't need her to compare me to my friend when I did it myself.

The truth is that we compare ourselves to imperfect people all the time. God did not call us to compete with one another but to be who He designed us to be. Unfortunately, we tend to focus on how ill-equipped we are versus how God truly sees us. We are God's workmanship, and there is no need to compete with what God did not give us. God gave Sherrell a beautiful voice to lift his praises. I could take voice lessons for a lifetime and never sing like her. However, to my knowledge, she has never written a book. The point is that even with our flaws, we are uniquely designed by God to accomplish our specific tasks. There is no need to compare ourselves to others, but we should evaluate ourselves against a perfect God.

Newsflash: the flesh is imperfect. There is no picture-perfect human on Earth. Adam and Eve are about as close as we will get as they were God's first blueprint of humanity. I am sure that Adam and Eve were physically flawless. They probably could have run for Eden's Mr. and Miss Universe pageant and won. However, even with their perfect bodies, they still made faulty decisions.

We know all too well the fall of Creation thanks to our forefather and mother. They had flawless bodies but inadequate spirits. They were probably as close to perfection as humans could obtain. Yet, with their most incredible physiques and beauty, they had a weak soul causing sin to enter the world.

Here is another newsflash; we *are* inadequate. Our flesh is sinful and insufficient as the dust it is made from. It has no value, yet we polish what many remove from their homes. If the dirt under our beds is worthless, what about our flesh? I have never seen valuable dust. Nor have I noticed signs that read dust for sale. We are flesh made from the dirt, having little value or worth; nonetheless, our spirits make us satisfactory before God.

YOUR FLESH IS NOT THE REAL YOU

God does not deal with our flesh but our spirit as our bodies operate through our hearts and minds. The body performs what our inner man commands. My mouth is an instrument that can either open to pray or to cuss you out. My hands can be tools to worship God, or I can use them to lay someone flat on their back. I can use my feet to dance for him or decide to twerk in the club. Our bodies only follow what's in our hearts. For Christians to be in tune with God, separating our outer and inner man must occur. We are so fixated on perfecting our flesh and desires that the real us is weak, feeble, and dying.

We tend to spend more time eating healthy versus reading God's word. We change our diets and nutrition rather than change our behaviors. We spend an hour at the gym when we can't spend an hour in prayer. We look at social media to alter our appearance when we can't search the Bible to change our mindset. The only part of ourselves that can be remotely perfect is within our Spirit, yet we tend to focus on something that can never be ideal.

Trust me; I get it. As I type this, I'm checking my Fitbit for steps, calculating my Weight Watchers points, and staring at an underutilized Peloton. Of course, I am doing this while attempting to ignore the big bag of chips in the cabinet. Yes, I'm in the fat-bulge fight with you, aiming for the best body I can obtain at my age. However, after writing all of this, I think, what's the point? Why reserve what is corruptible when I could just eat the chocolate chip cookie? And the chocolate cake and binge-eat all the chips I want. After all, you can't eat just one.

Probably because I wouldn't stop at the cookie, cake, or chips. As followers of Christ, we should take care of our bodies. Nevertheless, we should not consume our minds to reach the perfect physique. Instead, we should use that same energy and zeal to perfect who we are in Christ.

Jesus implored us to be perfect because God is perfect. This seems to be an outlandish request. How can we be perfect when we are part flesh? Our flesh is not of God (Gal 5:16 – 22). Yet, Jesus implored us to be perfect. I genuinely doubt that our God is lifting ten-ton weights when he holds the world in his hands. Nor do I believe he is in Heaven counting carbs and calories. He is already perfect. Therefore, if it is not through our physical frame, then perhaps we need to start working on improving our spiritual bodies.

When the psalmist says, "I am fearfully and wonderfully made," we tend to think about our natural being. As previously stated, God has created excellence in you. Every inch of your body was created and designed as God saw fit. God did not create defective people. We are indeed fearfully and wonderfully made, yet instead of focusing on our physical appearance, let's start thinking about our spiritual man.

We are the perfect workmanship of God, made in his image. However, what is the image of God? John believed that God is a spirit unconfined by a human body (John 4:24). Remember, as the temple of God, the nature of God dwells inside us. Therefore, when God spoke to the divine tribunal, saying, let us make man in our image, perhaps he spoke in spiritual terms and not physicality.

GOD IS A PERSON, BUT HE IS NOT HUMAN.

Throughout the Bible, we can see scriptures that indicate that God has characteristics of a person and even human features. Scripture suggests that God walked with Adam (Gen 3:8), wrestled with Jacob (Gen 32:28), and denied Moses' request to see his face but showed him his back (Ex 33:18 – 23). I've never had any of these encounters with God, but I know he talks with me, proving that he is a person, but how does he take on a human form?

Many theologians believe this is explained through theophany, in which God manifests himself in human form for our minds[1]. When Jesus came to Earth as Emmanual, God prepared him a body (Heb 10:5). If Jesus was already human, why couldn't he come to Earth in his form, growing into his nature from infancy to adulthood? Perhaps, the splendor of Jesus was too much for human eyes to see, or maybe because before his incarnation, Jesus was a spirit.

We know that Jesus was both human and divine, as this dual nature is supported by his virgin birth (Matt 1:18). We also know before his embodiment, he was the Word (John 1:1). It is unknown, however, whether Jesus possessed a human form before his Earthly descent, but we know he existed. Therefore, if God *is* a spirit and if Jesus *was* human only when he came to Earth, then could it be said that we are fearfully and wonderfully made in the Spirit?

John said that our worship is done in spirit and truth (John 4:24). I can use my body to praise and worship God, but my flesh cannot worship. God is a spirit; when we connect to him through worship, our heart worships, not our physical bodies. When God breathed his breath into Adam, he gave us both physical and spiritual life. Yes, God constructed our natural bodies, which are defected by scars and disease, yet our spirits are made perfect through a relationship with God.

Our natural bodies die daily as our spiritual man is consistently renewed with life. Ironically, as we die, we live. Since this is the case, how much time do we attempt to perfect our spiritual selves? For example, we can look in the mirror and see a healthy human being for the most part. However, what if God gave us a spiritual-looking glass? What would we see? Would we see a fit

---

1. Fairchild, "How Did God Appear to Man in the Old Testament?", lines 1 – 3.

person, strong and mighty, ready for spiritual warfare? Or would we see a fragile, broken corpse prepared for burial?

Our Spirit is made perfect, yet we allow our flesh to corrupt what is incorruptible. Our sinful flesh will return to the dust one day, and our spirit will gain either everlasting life or death. That's our choice. God provided us with bodies for his divine purpose to do his good works. Our inner man, the real us, is for our benefit as we work towards an eternal inheritance. Too bad some of God's Creation works towards death, but those who live uprightly will live forever as our spirit is fearfully and wonderfully made.

So what does that mean? What does the Bible mean when it says that God created us in fear and wonder? Obviously, God was not afraid of making man, nor did he wonder how he would do it. After all, he is God. Yet, the word fear derives from the Hebrew word *yare*, meaning "to be in awe of, reverence, respect, and honor.[2]" Now, I am about to blow your mind. When God says we are fearfully made, he looks at us in astonishment. Imagine creating something that came out better than you thought it could be. That's how God views his children. He sees the best qualities he has placed inside us and is amazed because we turned out better than he could *even* expect.

GOD IS IN AWE OF YOU.

Frequently, we are amazed by God. However, have you ever thought that he is amazed by you? I know, mind-boggling, right? Still, I believe that an omniscient God is sometimes surprised by our actions and deeds: the good, the bad, and the ugly. I know some holier-than-thou person will argue that nothing takes God by surprise. Of course, he knows everything; however, I do believe that when we act in his will, he is amazed because he gave us free choice to choose. Therefore, I can't help but feel that God looks at his Creation in amazement when we please him and bewilderment

---

2. McMenamin, "What Does Reverence Mean, and How to Practice Daily Reverence", lines 22 – 26.

when we don't. Nevertheless, I genuinely believe that God takes delight in his children.

God created us for his glory. If we were made to glorify God, do you genuinely believe God would make something ineffectual or useless to provide him praise? Of course not. We are fearfully and wonderfully made to be great instruments of praise, vessels of worship, and worthy of every spiritual blessing he provides. All of Creation was created for his glory, yet we are the ones that can openly proclaim his worth to the world. Think about it. Why would God create a faulty instrument to declare his magnificent splendor? Nevertheless, we are fearfully and wonderfully made of good quality, of good stock. We are fearfully and wonderfully made through the spirit of the living God.

The best part is that his masterpiece, which started thousands of years ago, is not yet finished. God knew us before time, and thousands of years later, we are formed. Still, God's work is not yet complete. He continues to mold and shape our inner man into perfection every day. I know we tend to see ourselves as inadequate, wondering if we are even worthy of being a part of God's plan. However, we are a significant element of God's masterpiece. Outwardly, we may not resemble much. Again, I still would love to get that tummy tuck and BBL, but inwardly I am a work of art. The most magnificent blueprint of God's divine plan.

This floppy body is imperfect, flawed, scarred, ugly, and fat. And it's okay because God designed every stretch mark and cellulite on this body. And as unattractive as they are, they are there for a purpose. If my anti-cellulite cream works, then so be it. If it doesn't, then God wants it there for a purpose. At this point, it does not matter because my concern is my inner man. However, I still would like the excess fat off my body. You hear that, Lord, I need the fat removed. Amen.

We may be unsatisfied with our bodies. However, it is more important that God is satisfied with our souls. Our bodies were perfectly designed yet are feeble, returning to the dust. It is our spirit that is fearfully and wonderfully made. Therefore, we should work on our spiritual health more than we care about our physical. And for me, I am going to eat the chocolate chip cookie.

Chapter 7

I am the salt of the Earth.

"Ye are the salt of the earth: but if the salt have lost his savour, wherewith shall it be salted? it is thenceforth good for nothing, but to be cast out, and to be trodden under foot of men."

—Matthew 5:13

"PLEASE, PASS THE SALT."

No cook wants to hear that their food is underseasoned. Next to burning food, not having enough salt can be considered one of the top cardinal cooking sins. I think I'd rather burn my food instead of lacking flavor. Burnt food could be blamed on carelessness. *Sorry, the phone was ringing. Someone was at the door. I thought I saw an alien.* However, there is no excuse for not having enough salt. How could you possibly justify that? What could you perhaps say? *The alien, I thought I saw, took the salt while I was at the door burning my food.* Again, I rather believe that ET came for a visit instead of my food lacking seasoning.

I've never said that I was the best cook in the world. Although I am far from the worst, one thing is guaranteed; salt will be added to my food. Sometimes, a little too much. I just like to sprinkle a little in my water, a touch on my vegetables, a dab over my meats, and pretty much anything I'm about to put in my mouth. I even put it on certain fruits to bring out the flavor. Trust me; salt is a cook's best friend as it appears that every dish requires it.

Think about it, have you ever noticed the nutritional facts in foods? Sodium is usually present. Before my chemist daughter corrects me by saying sodium and salt aren't the same, I paid attention enough in high school chemistry to know that salt is a significant component of the chemical element. So, theoretically, salt is everywhere. Seafood, beverages, bread, desserts, it doesn't matter, salt can be found. No wonder this seasoning is the most widely used in the world.

We can't deny that salt is highly utilized. But why? Well, let's think of all the reasons why we use salt. Of course, we use it to season our foods; however, I recently underwent dental surgery where a daily saline rinse made the difference between tolerable discomfort and excruciating torture. I also noticed that my morning breath had disappeared because of my saltwater routine. We can also use it for constipation, an ingrown toenail, tired feet, and a runny nose; you know, all the gross things our bodies go through that we don't want to talk about.

I know I'm about to sound like an article in Good Housekeeping, but salt has other unknown household uses. For example, salt is a good cleaning agent to remove wine stains from carpets, freshen refrigerators, and quickly dispose of a broken egg. If you have a carton of milk getting closer to the expiration date, just use salt to extend the shelf life. It can also be used in the garden to kill weeds and eliminate pesky bugs. Speaking of annoying insects, sprinkling salt around window and door frames can help stop the ants from marching one by one; hurrah, hurrah! Salt is a viable element with multiple uses and seems to be everywhere. However, Good Housekeeping never explained why Jesus called believers the salt of the earth.

Indeed, we are multi-faceted as we perform numerous deeds for the Kingdom of God, but I doubt that is what Jesus meant. Nor

I AM THE SALT OF THE EARTH.

do I think he called us the salt of the Earth because we are everywhere. Christians can indeed be found on every continent, as I am sure there is a believer in Antarctica freezing in the name of science. Yet, I doubt that is what Jesus meant as well. So, why would the Son of God disvalue believers to be compared to something that costs no more than a dollar?

Why not gold? Why couldn't we be the glimmering gold of the world versus something as practical and lowly as salt? No doubt, salt is a viable mineral, but so is gold. Gold sparkles and shimmers and seems to be more valuable and prestigious. I never heard of anyone giving their significant other a pint of salt for Valentine's Day. Try it, and I can guarantee the next holiday they will spend alone.

As I pondered this question, the only notion I could fathom was preservation. Salt preserves meats, and I could only assume that Jesus called us the salt of the Earth to maintain this world. That sounded well and good until I began to consider the world. This place is merely a pit stop in our spiritual journey. We are not of this Earth. Like the alien who made me burn my food, I am simply an extraterrestrial—just a mere visitor. Why would I care about preserving this world when it is not my final resting place?

Sure, I do my part to recycle and maintain its beauty. I even started getting into lawn care in my old age. I've learned more about pruning and mulching than I care to know. Yet, I doubt that Jesus meant for all Christians to become tree huggers and Arbor Day fanatics. I'm sure he wants us to care for what he gave us, but not to the point of preservation. The question remains as to why Jesus would call us the salt of the Earth if this place would one day fade away.

That's right, Heaven and Earth will one day be gone, poof, never to exist again (Matt 24:35). However, God's word will never fade, making it even harder to understand why Jesus would want us to preserve this world. John saw a new Heaven and a new Earth, which means protecting this one is a little idiotic. If we are getting a better world, then why am I salt? Just thinking about it is making me salty. Again, we could have been the glistening gold of this world and not a common mineral. Salt is for preservation, and the only thing that will persist is God's Word and our spiritual man.

Ureka! Our spiritual man *is* eternal. It was like the Holy Spirit smacked me over the head with the obvious answer. Jesus did not mean for us to preserve something as trivial as this world. Again, this physical world will be gone forever. However, our souls will continue to last, and the only way that we can ensure eternal life is by standing steadfast in God's word. It took me a while, but I finally understood the reference to salt. Jesus called believers the salt of the Earth to keep everyone's spiritual man from eternal death. Gold is radiant, but salt is sustainable.

Ironically, our spiritual man *will* outlast Heaven and Earth. I know it's hard to comprehend we will survive a planet that has stood for billions of years, but we will. Unlike Heaven and Earth, our spirit is everlasting, either inheriting eternal delight or despair. Since we will outlive both of these places, it is the job of believers to salt the world with the Word of God. As the salt of the Earth, we have a God-given duty to build the Kingdom of God by preserving the souls of man and leading them to eternal life versus death.

Salting this Earth is a significant task that Jesus gave to each believer. Think about it. He has so much confidence in you that he believes you can convert and preserve people's spiritual man. Just as Jesus spoke to the ordinary people at the Mount, he believes that you are of great worth and value. Gold is important, but salt has more purposes than gold during biblical times and even today. Argumentatively, we may want to be referred to as a valuable mineral like gold. Yet, it is safe to say we can live without gold, but we cannot live without salt. Therefore, this world cannot live without the salt that you provide.

God saw you as a valuable part of preserving this world. People need you to help them survive their spiritual journey. How can others not become contaminated by this world without the spiritual salt you provide? Years ago, people used salt to preserve foods. However, you are the salt of this world to stop the spiritual rot of sin. You are needed within the body of Christ to combat the rotten stench of corruption and spiritual decay with your saltiness.

I AM THE SALT OF THE EARTH.

You are indeed the salt of the Earth, but you cannot lose your flavor. If you are not careful, you can lose your spiritual spice. Mainly there are two types of salt, refined salt (table salt) and natural salt, found in lakes and oceans. Contrary to popular belief, table salt can expire and has a shelf life of about five to seven years, after which it loses its potency. It can still be used, but it is not as effective. The only salt that is indefinite is natural salt.

Unfortunately, as believers, we can become contaminated, losing our efficiency in the body of Christ. Natural salts have lasting power because it maintains their original minerals, as table salt is enriched with iodine. Here I go again with my antics; however, we must keep our God-given nature if we want to last. The truth is that salt, when kept appropriately, can last forever. Yet, when it becomes tainted, it loses its effectiveness. We believers cannot let our salt become polluted by strongholds, weights, or sin. However, we must stand firm, being saturated within the Spirit of God, to ensure that our salt can last.

What good is salt if it loses its flavor? Any cook worth their salt (pun intended) will tell you there is no reason to season your food with stale salt. It is ineffectual and has no use. Now, I would never tell you that you are good for nothing. I think you are great. However, Jesus said that if your salt is flavorless, you are about as worthless as the dirt we walk on. Again, I think you are terrific, but you are a water-downed Christian if you aren't salty.

No one wants to eat bland mashed potatoes. They are hard to swallow without a good dash of salt. So, why would we think that Jesus wants tasteless followers? It's about time that we check our seasoning. Well seasoned food makes us move and do a happy dance. While poorly flavored food leaves a bad taste in our mouths.

Are we a bad taste in God's mouth? Are we as bland as unsalted mashed potatoes? Is God looking at our stale, dull enthusiasm for him and reaching for other salted vessels to take our place? I know it's hard to swallow like those unseasoned potatoes, but the fact is that we can't afford to lose our saltiness.

Our salt is valuable as it is multi-purposeful. To my surprise, there are several uses for salt, with the principal benefits being preservation, cleaning, and healing. We are here to preserve the world but also to help cleanse it from unrighteousness and heal contrite and broken hearts. God has placed much confidence in our saltiness, but how will we fulfill this task? How can we talk to unbelievers who seem deaf to the truth? How can we heal sick people when they don't want to recover? Conversion always has been a challenge in Christianity. However, Apostle Paul said we would meet this challenge through wisdom and speech seasoned with salt (Col 4:4 – 6).

Well, what in the world is salty speech? Conversations seasoned with salt means that our persuasion should produce preservation versus destruction. Let's think about it with natural salt. Often we tend to focus on the negative aspects of salt in our diets, primarily when we use too much. However, salt has excellent benefits, such as helping digestion, removing toxins, and aiding in rehydration. Coincidentally, these same advantages are needed when we communicate with unbelievers. We need to help them absorb God's Word, show them how to remove the toxicity of sin, and teach them how to become saturated within the Spirit. Yet, when we focus merely on their lives' negative aspects, we do more harm than good. Therefore, when we talk with non-Christians, we should focus on the positive aspects of holiness versus the restrictions of a holy life.

THERE IS POWER IN YOUR SALTY CONVERSATION.

As a teenager, the most powerful phrase I heard from Christians was, " I shouldn't." I shouldn't wear this; I shouldn't wear that. I shouldn't say this, or I shouldn't say that. I heard it so much that I wondered was there any good in me. Unlike teens my age, I didn't overly engage in underage drinking, didn't attend parties without my parent's knowledge, and was a good student. I never got into trouble. In my teacher's eyes, I was considered a perfect student.

Once, I even begged for after-school detention just to have a story about getting into trouble before I ended my high school career. Unfortunately, my "after-school detention" turned into an after-school party, but I tried. My teachers thought I was an outstanding student, as did my guidance counselors and principals. I was a good child, yet the chorus of "I shouldn't" always outweighed the positive attributes given to me outside of the church.

You would have thought I was the most rebellious child in the world. Sure, I didn't feel like attending Friday night youth services, especially when my alma mater played our rivals, but I did. After the game, I loaded up all the youth and headed straight to church. I wasn't the only one who missed half the service, but you would have thought I was the ring leader instead of the person rushing them off the field.

I participated in church. I was faithful to the choir and was always there for rehearsals. I took part in church plays and programs. Read poems for Black History Month and even acted out a few. I sang solos when I was forced and traveled with my choir when I wasn't. I did my part. Yet, no one said anything about those things; it was always:

"Your skirt is too short."

"You shouldn't wear nail polish."

"Your heels are too high."

"What's that on your lips?"

"That's too many bracelets."

You would have thought I was the church's Jezebel, and I guess I was compared to the other girls who *always* did the right thing and looked like pilgrims fresh off the Mayflower. I received some very salty talk; however, what did it produce?

The answer: a young girl who always felt unworthy because of how she talked and what she wore.

It only made me want to rebel against everything my church said was wrong about me. I thought, 'If everything I did was terrible, then let's see how bad I could become.' My skirts became shorter, my lipstick became brighter, and my heels rose higher. They were good Christians; of course, I didn't want them to have inappropriate opinions about me; therefore, I decided to prove them right. My skirts were short, my lipstick was unacceptable, and my heels were made for the streets. Yet, because I didn't want them to be liars, I did *exactly* what they thought.

Christians must first give the good news before the dire consequences. The salt I received as a youth could have been destructive. We know that God's Word is not grievous or hard to consume, yet it must be done in stages. You wouldn't give a baby a ribeye, no more than you should point out all the sins of an unbeliever. Like too much salt could be fatal, so could criticizing an unbeliever's lifestyle. We can't scare people to Christ because we know all sinners will have their personal tanning beds in a lake of fire. However, we can tell them about God's love as love always overcomes fear.

DON'T DISCOUNT YOUR SALT.

People sometimes attempt to dilute your flavor, measuring your value against theirs. Every believer is salted and seasoned with the Word of God. Some are well-seasoned, while others are slightly spiced. You must measure your salt in quality and not quantity. Of course, we all should grow in grace; some will grow faster than others. This does not mean your salt is less valuable or useless than theirs. Your salt has value, and you must always stay firm in your saltiness.

Too often, we can become intimidated by Christians who seem well-versed in scripture and biblical theology. We feel our salt's worth is less valuable, yet that is far from true. As we grow in Christ, so does our salt. We may not be able to quote scriptures or speak prophetically, and we may even need to use the index to find if Joel is in the Old or New Testament. Yet, the salt you possess can add flavor to someone's dull and mundane life. Don't measure your salt against other believers, as the amount of salt in your spiritual vessel is essential and needed in and outside the body of Christ.

Your salt can make a difference in a flavorless, dehydrated world that needs spiritual healing. God has called you the salt of

I AM THE SALT OF THE EARTH.

the Earth because you are valuable seasoning to help preserve, clean, and heal this world. Daily, we are confronted with distressing news of school killings, war, and racial inequality. Our news cast and social media feeds are filled with horrific daily updates of our dying world. It's depressing, and even though your salt may not change this world, it can change someone. You never know what a friendly smile or words of encouragement can do to aid in making someone's life a little less distasteful. As a child of God, you must do your part to help season the world with the Word of God. You can't be stingy with your seasoning, nor can you lose your flavoring. However, you must continue to pass on your salt.

Chapter 8

I am the light of God.

"Ye are the light of the world. A city that is set on a hill cannot be hid".

—Matthew 5:14

A FEW CHRISTMASES AGO, I received a charm bracelet from my co-teacher that said, "be the light." I felt horrible because my gift to her had no thought whatsoever. It was my unoriginal Bath and Body Works go-to gift, tucked neatly in a Dollar Tree bag. However, my co-worker presented me with a beautiful piece of jewelry with an even more beautiful inspirational message: *be the light*.

It was so fitting because we were both teachers inspiring impressionable students daily. Therefore, I vowed to be my students' light, the best teacher possible. However, as I peered at the bracelet, I only thought of the educational message, not the spiritual one. I thought it was a cute little phrase given by a cute little co-worker, and I would go on my cute little way.

I wore my bracelet every day until I noticed the once white background had faded, just about as quickly as my motivation. By March, I was dreaming of summer. Spring break was around the corner, but I needed more than a week to free myself from those unruly children. A week, seven days could not heal me from the

I AM THE LIGHT OF GOD.

constant demands of "sit down," "be quiet," "stop talking," or my signature phrase, "I'm about to jack you up."

I'm sure you've heard of "one bad apple spoils the bunch." Well, I had several bad apples rotten to the core. And what do you do with rotten apples? You toss them out or, in my case, remove them from your class. However, suspension at the elementary level seems as farfetched as using a rotten apple to make apple pie. I had broken up numerous fights, stopped World War III from happening, and was even called a female dog. Ironically, I've only been called this once in my life by a drunk thug in college, but here I was, taking this insult from a scrawny eleven-year-old.

I had had enough. There was no way I could survive my first year of teaching. I had been an educator for over a decade, but college students were different. Teaching college was seemingly effortless. I would lecture, discuss, grade a few papers, crack some jokes, and collect my check—nothing to it. However, teaching children meant that you were not only an educator, but a nurse, custodian, guidance counselor, coach, referee, entertainer, technician, and the list could go on. But most of all, you are a foster parent for eight hours a day, and I had my own child to deal with. So, put a fork in me because I was done. I had loved every one of my students, but there was no way I would finish the school year without catching a case. Yet, I put my big girl panties on and persevered until schools closed due to COVID-19.

March 12th, 2020, was my worst day of teaching and learning ever. It was our Pi Day Celebration, and I had spent roughly 20 percent of my meager teacher's check buying supplies to celebrate the quotient of circumference and diameter. Now, I'm thinking how stupid of me. I could have just given them a few worksheets and called it a day. But, no. I had to be the teacher who had devoted her entire weekend to preparing fun, engaging, rigorous lessons.

Who knew that bubble solution would be spilled over the whole classroom, that hula hoops would be used for their *actual* purposes, and that the students would break most of my materials by the first block? Well, this girl didn't know because if I had prior knowledge of this fiasco, I would have just given them a test while sipping my coffee and looking at the newspaper.

But, peace this day was out of the question. I had chosen verbal violence. Trust me, I didn't want to yell, but my normal teacher voice could not be heard over all the fun. So, my next move was to turn out the lights. This would generally signal them to stop in their tracks, but they continued slipping and sliding over the soapy solution. My last attempt was to flicker the lights off and on, but this only made my classroom look like a midnight rave. My next step was to yell. So, I yelled and continued to scream until the yelling felt good.

My students stopped spilling bubble solution long enough to see their teacher's disappointment. All of them froze in their tracks as I took inventory of the room. It was a mess. Broken hula hoops, circle disks, soapy floors, tossed rulers, and yards of string decorated my once-organized environment. Usually, I would insert an excellent lecture to make my students think about their actions. However, this time, I didn't have the energy. All I could think about was the money and time spent planning a great lesson that had been tossed aside, like the materials I had given my students. There was nothing more that could be done. My students were summoned to their seats to sit in silence, watching as I tried to salvage the remaining materials for the next class.

No words needed to be said; witnessing their bougie teacher on hands and knees cleaning the floor seemed to do the trick. There I was in dress slacks and my blouse wiping the floor and picking up broken items. My actions were speaking louder than my words, and I made a spectacle. A few head shakes, a little dramatic tosses to the trash, add some huffs and puffs, and my students looked guilty and disappointed in themselves.

Good! They should feel disappointed! No one said a word when they left my room. Perhaps they were terrified, or maybe they saw the real tears swelling in my eyes. Either way, no words were spoken.

My students wouldn't even look at me in the hallway throughout the day. No one saluted me with their customary goodbyes and hugs. Instead, they shuffled quickly past me with lowered heads and guilty consciences. Good! They should feel embarrassed. After all, I was a great teacher. I gave my all, and my all was good enough. They were the ones that were acting like little brats. I was glad they didn't speak. Happy they didn't peer my way. I was ecstatic that it was Thursday and had one more day to go until the weekend. I had won the battle and felt great until I realized I would probably never see my babies again.

The announcement came. The school was closing due to Covid-19. Hurray! I remember vividly doing my own ticker-tape parade, throwing ungraded assignments in the air. I quickly gathered my belongings, running into the hallway and singing, "Schools out for the Summer." Of course, it was only supposed to be two weeks, but I knew God was intervening on my behalf. There was no way I was going to make it until June. My faith was that we were not coming back. My co-worker hugged me because I looked defeated, which I was. Leaving the school, I would have done cartwheels if I wasn't so fat, but I felt incredible joy: no more lesson planning, no more meetings, and most of all, no more students.

Wait, no more students.

It had hit me. School had ended, and I wouldn't see my babies tomorrow. Maybe even never again. There would be no more funny antics, no more heartfelt drawings, or the occasional "I love you." It had all ended, and I didn't get the opportunity to say goodbye. I was utterly crushed. Despite my last day, those children meant everything to me, and their last impression was a frantic screeching woman who told them I never wanted to hear them call me their favorite teacher ever again. Unfortunately, I got my wish.

Even with them making me gain stress weight and a few gray hairs, I missed my students. Every day, I would think about them. I would even break social isolation, heading to the local grocery store and seeking them out. That worked as I saw one or two, but I never got too close. I hid behind my mask because I was sure they didn't want to see me. After all, I didn't want to see them on our last day and felt the feeling was mutual.

However, after a few weeks, I decided I would be strong and contacted them through email. I put the bait out there and prepared for the silence. I thought no one would respond. However, the emails, text messages, and friend requests were rolling in to my surprise. I was amazed at how much they missed me. Even the young man, who called me everything but a child of God, had a noticeable grin when he saw me. The other one texted me frequently. To my surprise, they didn't recall how crazy I acted on our last day; they only seemed to remember that I cared throughout the year.

Looking at the faded message on my bracelet, I remembered I was their light. As their math teacher, I taught them about integers, ratios, and fractions, yet it was much more. I had formed a relationship with them that went beyond the confines of the classroom. I attended football and soccer games, stayed after school for unpaid tutoring sessions, talked to them about being respectful young men, built my young ladies' self-esteem, and was there for them every moment I could spare. I was a temporary lamp shining in their life.

I cared about my students, and ironically, they cared about me. Over the next two years, I saw several of them who said I made a difference in their lives. Students who never liked math were now excelling in arithmetic. Girls who felt unattractive began to blossom because I told them they were beautiful daily. My boys asked me to come to their football games, recalling how I was their biggest cheerleader during recess. However, we reunited again as I am currently teaching them at the local high school. It was astonishing they had remembered, and tears filled my eyes when I was told I was still their favorite teacher. Again, I was their light.

Often we do not think about the impact that we have on others. I know I didn't. I just loved my babies, and that love made the difference. Sometimes we have no clue how brilliantly our light shines throughout someone else's darkness. However, there is a spark inside of you that cannot be easily distinguished. Never think that who you are does not matter. After all, who would have thought that a simple carpenter's child would one day save the entire world?

Jesus Christ is the light of this world, and God gave us this same title. Incredibly, we can share this name with God's Son. Like the sun is the natural light that separates our nights from day, the Son of God is the spiritual light separating our lives from good and evil. Since we are joint-heirs with Christ, we have the same title as light ambassadors of God.

Of course, there is no way that the moon and the stars can compete with the sun. The sun is placed in the center of our universe. It is our primary source of energy and light. I don't even want to think about what will happen when the sun stops shining. I prefer to be in heaven preparing my white horse for battle. Nevertheless, the sun is still placed and continues to shine along with the stars and the moon. The sun still needs those light sources to brighten the night, just like the Son of Man needs us to be light to decrease the darkness of sin.

We cannot allow our light to be snuffed out no more than saying we don't need the stars and the moon. We are the world's light that aids the Son to shine bright. What would happen if we allowed our light to go out? I believe the world would be in worst shape than we could ever imagine. We are already facing end-time revelations, with wars, natural disasters, and nations against nations (Matt 24: 6 – 7). If we allow our light to go out, we are merely ineffectual lamps decorating the world without purpose.

To me, there is nothing more frustrating than trying to turn on a light that does not light. It infuriates me because it is not doing its job. The job of a lamp is to turn on, producing light. When that doesn't happen, I quickly begin troubleshooting. I make sure it's connected to the electrical socket. If that does not work, I then change the bulbs. I even go to the electrical panel to switch the breakers. After my failed troubleshooting attempts, I determined that the light no longer serves its purpose. Therefore, I either keep it or trash it.

I wonder if that's what God does when our light seems to flicker. Does he troubleshoot to determine the problems with our shine? Or does he find another willing lamp to light the way? I am unsure because I keep my decorative lamps but throw out the bulbs that don't work.

Maybe when our light goes dim, God tries to replace our bulbs or, in this case, our motivation. Now, I don't care how holier than thou you may be; every Christian has had a dim light once and a while. We tend to lose our enthusiasm for Christian living. It does not mean we are any less saved or satisfied with God. It means God has to bring a new trial, tribulation, or blessing to reunite our flame.

As Christians, we are the light of the World. During the sermon on the Mount, Jesus gave two similitudes within the beatitudes, comparing believers to salt and light. I think understanding how we are light is much easier than understanding how we are Christian salt. Salt has multiple purposes. However, light has one significant one: to help us see. When Jesus compared us to light, he meant for believers to help those blinded by the truth through our deeds and actions. Yet, we cannot overly brighten the way to the end of invisibility.

Sometimes, I believe we as Christians come off as so radical that it deters people from Christ. We look more like snake handlers than faithful followers. It's like driving and being blinded by the sun. The sun is there to brighten our way, but sometimes it makes it harder to see. As Christians, we must use wisdom to determine how bright our light needs to shine in certain situations.

No Christian enters a restaurant, passes by the bar, and starts speaking in tongues to those on the barstools. No more than we start laying hands on the person who asks for a pack of Marlboros at the grocery store. Instead, we shine our light by being courteous to the waitress, taking our cart back even if it's raining, and saying a small prayer for God to bless those we contact. God commands that we shine through the darkness, but as believers, we cannot shine so bright that people don't see Christ.

Now there are times when it will take some people to be blinded by the light. Paul is an excellent example. He encountered Jesus and lost his vision for three days but look what he gained.

I am the light of God.

Jesus is that blazing light; we can't try to outshine God. He doesn't need us to knock someone off their beast. He needs us to brighten the way to him so he can do it.

Try this exercise with me. Close your eyes and then place your hands over them. There is complete darkness. Now, keep your eyes closed and remove your hand. Notice how there is light attempting to penetrate through your eyelids? Light is stronger than darkness. Where light is, darkness cannot exist. Therefore, you have to be that light that rages against the dimness of this world. No matter how depressing a situation is, there is always hope because you are there. The shadow of darkness cannot remain when you are around. You are called to shine as you have no idea how a simple gesture can change the trajectory of someone's life.

While traveling to work one day, I was highly depressed, borderline suicidal. I was not ready to end my life, but a car accident would have been more than welcomed. As I contemplated whether to die or not to die, I recognized a woman walking along the highway. To my surprise, it was a member of my church. She gleefully jumped and waved, brightly smiling as I passed by. Then it happened; tears ran down my face. She only had been exercising, but little did she know that she gave me hope because I saw the light of God in her.

I hate to think of the coincidental impact that would have occurred if my sister was not on that highway. I was about to travel over a seventeen-mile bridge, and one wrong decision could have ended my life. Later, I revealed this incident to her, and she only smiled. She didn't share any prophetic messages about why she was far from her usual walking route. Nevertheless, she simply grinned and said, "I was just happy to see you." I am forever grateful that she chose to shine that day versus allowing the cares of life to extinguish her light. If she hadn't, my light might have been removed forever.

That's the choice that we must make as the children of God. Are we willing to outshine the darkness even when our world seems glum? Are we ready to illuminate the characteristics of God even when we want to give up? That's what it means to be light.

Light has no other choice but to shine throughout the darkness. That's what it is made to do, cast out darkness and give way to sight. In the dark, we stumble; however, God's light leads us on the correct path.

Unfortunately, our adversary has tricked many into walking in the dark because they have become accustomed to it. Each night, nature calls, and either I or my dog must answer. I often close my eyes as I can easily navigate to the bathroom. I know the layout of my home to steer past furniture and proceed to my nightly destination. I have done this for roughly nine years, and I think I've only stumped my toe once because I am familiar with the obstacles in my house.

Then it happened. I recently tripped over a dumbbell peeking out from under my bed. I didn't fall, nor did I hurt myself. I was more alarmed because I didn't anticipate anything in my path.

Unfortunately, that's how it is when we walk in darkness. We feel secure enough to continue our journey without anticipating obstacles in our way. We have become so accustomed to the dark we've learned how to maneuver through it in the spirit but are still blind to many of life's challenges.

We know the trials before us, yet instead of entirely avoiding them by turning on our heavenly light switch, we rather fumble around the strongholds and fall over challenges we hadn't expected. God did not call us to fumble feebly in the dark, attempting to find our way. Yet, he said he would be a lamp onto our feet, a light onto our path (Ps 119:105). When God has paid your light bill, there is no need to sit in the dark.

Satan disguises himself as the angel of light; unfortunately, many are walking in a deceptive glow. They think everything is fine, yet they are on a destructive path. Therefore, as the children of God, we must stay connected to the light source. Jesus is the light source and has called us to come and walk in the light (John 3:19-20, Ephesians 5:8). Walking in the light of God makes us joint-heirs with Christ to become the light of God (Matt 5:14-16). We cannot function in a false light, but always ensure that the true light of God ignites because it is within you.

I AM THE LIGHT OF GOD.

Remember the childhood song, "This little light of mine; I'm going to let it shine." As children, we would bellow out these lyrics. Granted, it might not be in your current playlist queue, but let's take a moment to determine if your light is still shining. What turned off your light? Was it continued failures? Broken dreams, relationships that floundered. Something in life always seems to come to attempt to extinguish your flame. However, your light is not insignificant or dull; you may just need to add more fuel to your furnace.

Incredibly, the children of the Almighty God are the ones that feel the most inadequate when we are the shining stars of this World. We are connected to the greatest power source in this universe, yet we see our light as dim. When we discount ourselves, we also reduce the illumination of God within our lives. Take into account a flashlight that produces a weak light. The flashlight still works and is sufficient to lead you to new batteries. No matter what circumstances you have encountered, your light is still active. Just take a moment to recharge it.

Revival is often needed for the children of God as our light can become impacted by our problems. Our light can be shining brightly one minute and snuffed out the next. However, we must renew ourselves through Jesus Christ when those situations arise. Life is hard, especially when darkness is all around. Nevertheless, our renewing comes from our faith. God's word is not merely printed on paper; it is alive and active, ready to rejuvenate your light.

God compared us to a city on a hill versus a countryside road in the boondocks, because we illuminate in the dark (Matt 5:14). Being from rural Virginia, where the only light is a few isolated homes and cars on the highway, I can assure you; that you will need a GPS to navigate at night. It's dark and lonely, with the only reflecting light in the darkness coming from a deer's eyes. You will likely miss my hometown traveling along Lankford Highway as it doesn't stand out. However, think about a city like Las Vegas. Flying above the state of Nevada, there is no way to miss Sin City.

The lights of Vegas illuminate from thousands of miles away. There is no way it can hide, but it glitters in the desert. Ironically, Las Vegas is not among the largest cities in America, but it still shines bright. In this notion, we are Las Vegas (minus the sin). As Christians, we are outnumbered. Yet, we cannot be hidden either. We must shine. No one can ever mistake us for unassuming towns when we are the illuminated city of God.

You are the brilliant light of this world that God ordained to shine bright for him. You cannot represent God in the darkness; however, you must arise and shine. You are more significant than the light sources of this world. There is nothing in this universe that can outshine you. You are more brilliant than the sun, have more twinkle than the most vibrant star, more luminosity than the fullest of moons. You are the light of God, so get ready to ignite and shine bright not like a diamond but as a child of the King.

Chapter 9

I am an overcomer.

> For whatever is born of God overcomes the world, and this is the victory that has overcome the world—our faith. Who is the one who overcomes the world, but he who believes that Jesus is the Son of God?
>
> —1 JOHN 5:4–5

ONE OF MY GREATEST life testimonies occurred while I was in college. I was on a big campus, full of hope, bursting with potential, ready to pursue my life's long dream of becoming a college graduate. I had made it, and so did my friends. We were excited to explore our new campus, ready and willing to take on the world. Then as the elevator doors opened, it seemed that reality hit, and my dreams were soaring down to the basement to be put in storage there forever.

Reality came in the form of three guys from our hometown. Somehow the news had surfaced that we, and when I say we, I mean new Shore girls, were on campus. I didn't recognize any of them, but somehow Tasha did. That was strange because Tasha and I ran in the same circles, and these guys were outside my circumference. Nevertheless, they were the unofficial welcoming party.

Apparently, they had graduated from our high school, yet their faces did not register. Our alma mater had less than seven hundred students, and I remembered each attractive guy's face; and one guy definitely should have been on my radar. Therefore, I knew they could not have been in school with me. They looked older, more mature. 'They must be graduate students', I thought. When I asked about this, they laughed and revealed they were seniors, super-duper seniors. They had graduated at least five years from our high school and had been in college during that time without expecting to graduate anytime soon.

Four years. That's how long it should take to graduate from college, four years. However, those guys made college a full-time career with part-time benefits. From our encounter, I realized that my institution had a meager on-time graduation rate of less than seven percent. As our welcoming party discussed the impossibilities of graduating on time, I decided I would not become an unpaid employee at ODU. I would not become a statistic. That night, praying on an unfamiliar bunk bed, I vowed that I would graduate in the allotted time, four years.

Unfortunately, I was already off to a poor start. I received the scores from my placement test, receiving high marks across the board, except for math. My uninspiring scores had placed me in a noncredited remedial math class during my first semester. I was horrible at arithmetic, but I knew that little course had caused me three credits. Before starting, I was behind, playing catch-up to retrieve those lost course hours. Yeah, I was already filling out my application for an extended stay in college.

Then I became pregnant. There I was, a sophomore in college and expecting. I was terrified and nearly lost what was left of my mind. The emotional damage of this ordeal is another story, yet the academic turmoil was a challenge. Leaving the campus I loved, I attended community college. No more freedom, no more hanging out with my friends, no more hopes of joining a sorority. I was shipped home to the little life I tried hard to escape. I had no job, no means of supporting myself, and the father was seven thousand miles away fighting in a war. However, I was still determined to get my education despite it all.

Miraculously, my college offered a distance learning program at my local community college, and most importantly, it provided my college major. I was so grateful, and my outlook was great during my time in the program. I was on track to graduate next year, or so I thought until my academic advisor called me into his office inquiring about graduation. He knew I had expectations of graduating in May; however, one look over his glasses made me question if this was even possible. He handed me my course outline, asking, "Are you sure?" My heart sank. It seemed I was not going to graduate in four years.

I sat in class, hoping this would be my last Fall semester as I prepared myself for the possibility of not graduating next May. I calculated my credits for months to ensure I would graduate on time. I took every course possible, even the late-night and weekend classes, to be sure I could graduate. At that moment, I wanted to give up as my mind returned to the conversation I had three years ago. Evidently, those guys, who were now my friends, had been right. I wouldn't graduate in four years, and I had never felt so defeated.

I couldn't believe that my calculations were off. I was horrible at math, but not that bad. There was no way that I wouldn't be able to graduate next year. I had been so careful to take every course offered, so diligent in ensuring I passed every class with a B or higher. There was no possible way that I could have been this wrong. So, I calculated my course hours repeatedly to be sure. Each time I analyzed my credits, I became more nervous. *It couldn't be. It honestly couldn't be.* With my last calculations in my hands, tears trickling down my face, I ran to my advisor, screaming, "I don't want to graduate in May; I want to graduate this year!"

I believe this is what Apostle John spoke about when he said that we are overcomers. There are times in our lives when we will face impossible obstacles. God does not always bring storms into our lives for disruption. Some storms are there to move things out of our path. This is why Apostle John implored believers to triumph over adversity and discouragement because God will turn everything around for our good.

Throughout the gospels, John spoke much about overcoming, probably more than any other disciple of God. So, I started wondering why John wrote so much about being an overcomer. It wasn't like John had a baby out of wedlock or was a habitual fornicator. So, what did John have to overcome truly?

I didn't know much about his backstory, but I knew he wasn't one of the bad boys of the gospel. After all, John didn't betray Jesus with a kiss. Sure he had his faults, as he didn't earn the nickname Son of Thunder by merely being meek and humble. However, there had to be more to him to speak so much about overcoming.

After attempting to dig up some dirt on John, I came up short. There were no major past misdeeds, as he was a follower of Christ before Jesus called him to become a fisherman of men. John was in his inner circle witnessing many miracles and following him even to the cross. Also, Jesus demonstrated confidence in him as he entrusted John to care for his mother after his death. So, it seemed that John, the beloved, was squeaky clean. He didn't sell Jesus out for any silver or deny him. So, why did John speak so eagerly about being an overcomer when it appeared he had little to overcome?

As I continued studying John, I realized he had a few unfavorable moments. One was when Jesus rebuked him for attempting to prevent a man from casting out demons (Luke 9:49 – 50; Mark 9:38 – 41). Jesus also stopped John and his brother from intending to rain fire on a Samaritan village simply because they were less than gracious hosts (Luke 9:51–56). Lastly, another not-so-shining moment occurred when John's mother inquired if her sons could sit directly beside Jesus in the Kingdom of Heaven (Matt 20:20 – 27; Mark 10:35 – 45).

Talk about being a momma's boy. Maybe Salome needed to overcome being a doting mother, as those seats are probably preserved for Elijah, Moses, or Paul. Think about it, John, you couldn't even pray with him for one hour. These incidences seem minor, but it appears that John and maybe his mother needed to defeat some undesirable qualities. Ironically, these are the traits we tend to discount when discussing being an overcomer.

Often, we equate being an overcomer to conquering temptations and sins. Most assuredly, through our Lord and Savior, Jesus Christ, we have victory over our iniquity. However, we limit our status as overcomers when solely focusing on sin. It's easy to admit needing to conquer greed, lust, and pride. Sins are easy focal points we can pinpoint; however, there are attributes in our personalities that we may need to beat. As Christians, we neglect our not-so-shining characteristics because they aren't sins. Yet, they are unfavorable wrinkles in our spiritual garments that need some smoothing.

Remember how I said I don't like cleaning and probably never will? Well, we can add ironing to that list. Matter-of-fact, I despise taking out an ironing board and even plugging up the monstrous thing. It might stem from being burned with one when I was five, but regardless genuinely, I'm not too fond of it. Even when I iron, I tend only to get the major wrinkles out, leaving smaller ones. I always say, "that's good enough," as I gather my clothes to throw them on, creating more wrinkles.

Honestly, I don't want to admit it, but that's how I am in the spirit. I thought I was pristine because I didn't have any spots or stains of sin in my holy garments—no unpleasant smells in my spiritual attire. However, I overlooked my wrinkles. I discounted the creases, ridges, and folds. Let's just say I am not as altogether as I thought. Some characteristics of my personality need hard pressing; again, I'm not too fond of ironing. However, I'm learning to use my biblical starch to add more freshness and structure to resist further wrinkles. We must overcome these obstacles, whether self-doubt, people, anxieties, hatred, grief, or persecution. We must get the wrinkles out.

Paul implored Christians to alter their thinking to ensure our overcomer's mentality rather than having a worldly mindset. Before accepting Christ, our minds are filled with greed and lust, serving *our* purpose. Even when we are followers of Christ, we may continue to think this way. Yet, we must continually renew our minds daily to fulfill the perfect will of God.

John was a follower of Christian principles before meeting Jesus, yet he still suffered from anger and selfishness. Being the youngest of the disciples, his youthful thinking appeared to come under subjection. Immaturity caused him to act against the Samaritan village instead of understanding they weren't refusing Jesus but a Jew. Also, John's self-serving request to sit beside Christ in the Kingdom of Heaven demonstrated child-like arrogance. Therefore, John had to grow within the spirit to alter his quick temper into a devoted follower of Christ.

Indeed, John's transformation did not occur overnight, nor will ours. We must continuously stay on our spiritual journey to become overcomers. As believers, the first obstacle we defeat is sin. Ironically, it seems we can conquer sin more than the strongholds and weights we carry. Sin is a destroyer of unbelievers, but it appears that weights will be the downfall of those in Christ. The cares of life don't only weigh us down, but we hold on to them like life preservers when they are only dragging us further away from God, down to the drowning surface.

In reality, many Christians have become accustomed to the weights in their lives. They have been in situations so long that they wouldn't know how to function without them. As a therapist, I have witnessed firsthand clients who create problems once they are problem-free. Their lives are always centered around chaos or drama, so they self-sabotage because they can't operate without it.

We have also stayed steadfast in problems God attempts to loose us from as Christians. We become so entangled in our children, families, previous relationships, and past hurts that we tend to hold on to them when God has already untied us from those situations.

WE ARE MORE THAN CONQUERORS.

In reality, this phrase has become second nature to many Christians and has lost its power. We limit our role to mere conquerors;

when the Bible says we are *more than* victors. The phrase *more than* means we go beyond the previous comments that follow. It suggests that something is added to the last clause. For example, when we proclaim that God is *more than* enough, we know he supplies our needs. Yet, on the contrary, also gives us what we want, adding more to his provisions. Therefore, since God has called us to be more than conquerors, he improves our victors' roles. Unfortunately, some of us fall victim to being just conquerors while the rest are being conquered.

One of the first things we need to recognize is that before becoming more than a conqueror, there must first be an obstacle to defeat. As Christians, we must overcome our fears of trials and tribulations. Our adversary constantly strategizes against the body of Christ to find weaknesses in our spiritual limbs. That's nothing new, as we aren't ignorant of his devices. Yet, we are unaware of our victorious status over our adversary. Therefore, we should not become dismayed by the attacks of Satan. Instead, we should rejoice in knowing that each problem faced is already sealed with victory and is defeated.

Yet, because we spoke it, Satan already attempts to derail the plan of God. Satan knows that it is already done when we decree and declare anything. So he tries to come up against those things that we have spoken in Jesus' name because he knows the power that we possess, even if we don't recognize it.

Our world is filled with cowardly Christians afraid to face hardship. When faced with problems, we begin to fret, becoming fearful. Even though Jesus did not give us a spirit of fear, we can admit that we have been afraid at least once. We are human, and there is nothing wrong with feeling anxiety when trouble knocks at our door, but we cannot let it become a welcomed guest.

Once fear enters, it cripples us, causing us to lose sight of our victory. Instead of turning to prayer, we attend our own pity parties, even sending out invitations for others to join in our worry. Ultimately, we become weak soldiers on our battlefield, lifting our hands to surrender before raising our circumstances before God.

The good news is that we are *more than* conquerors. I am reminded of the story of King Jehosaphat. A tremendous military alliance marched against Judah, yet the Lord said that this battle was not Jehosaphat's but his. In return, Judah went out to fight the great army only to realize that the aligned nations fought among themselves, leaving King Jehosaphat's military victorious (2 Chr 20: 14 - 17).

Christians must believe that our battles are not ours but God's. Too many believers are attempting to fight wars that God has already won. We need to get off God's battlefield. Those who set out to conquer often have to strategize, prepare battle plans, setting up their victory. They strategically determine the best method of attack to claim their enemy's territory and then raid their lands. However, with God, we merely need to praise him through our trials. We aren't usually the ones that handle planning how we will be victorious. Our task is to give our situations to God and allow him to fight on our behalf.

Our victory is not in our battle, but it is in God. Paul admonished believers to be strong in the Lord and in the power of his might so we may stand against Satan (Eph 6:10 – 11). As Christians, we must put on the whole armor of God – the breastplate of righteousness, the belt of truth, the shield of faith, our feet covered in peace, the helmet of salvation, and the sword of the Spirit. This is how believers prepare for battle; we suit up and watch God fight for his people.

Paul never told believers to fight; he only admonished us to stand. We are more than conquerors. Conquerors go into combat, while believers go to God. Our victory is in our armor. Overcomers walk uprightly before God, always seeking peace and truth, covered by salvation while having faith in the Word of God. Too many Christians are fighting without their protection. We stand our ground by being fully armored in God. We don't have to strategize in our battles, nor do we have to fight through our circumstances. We are more than conquerors. We merely show up, step over the casualties of our situation, and claim our victory. We fight by standing.

In battle, we cannot become weak soldiers, afraid and delusional. However, we must stand our ground while God fights on our behalf. It's time to suit up. A frail army loses the fight before the war begins, yet a strong host claims victory before the fighting ends. Our struggle is not over, but neither is God. He is not done fighting for his children. Through our Lord and Savior Jesus Christ, we have overcome the world. We have been granted guaranteed victory every time.

THE PRINCIPLES OF AN OVERCOMER

Overcomers Recognize Defeat is not an Option

Overcomers often encounter obstacles; however, defeat is not an option. Life is challenging as the bible confirms the "fiery trials" that come to incinerate our faith. However, when we are suited up in God, we have the shield of faith that diverts every fiery dart that attempts to attack our trust in God. The Bible says that we can move mountains if we have faith the size of a mustard seed (Matt 17:20). Is our faith so small, so insignificant that it's tinier than one of the smallest seeds? Hilariously, one mustard seed can produce a tree that stands 20–30 feet high. That's the substance of our faith. We can plant it, causing it to grow, or put our faith shields into action. Either way, to be an overcomer, we have to possess faith, trusting that we will not be defeated.

We are not easily defeated.

Trials will come into our lives, and that's when our faith needs to be activated. There is nothing as final as the grave. Yet, the Son of God conquered a tremendous feat over our adversary through the power of faith. Jesus was confident that he would rise in victory if he surrendered to death. Death was not the end for Jesus, and it is not the end for you. Sure, there may be dead circumstances in your life that seem buried six feet deep. However, we are joint heirs with Christ and heirs to victory. We just have to believe it. Every obstacle encountered must be overcome. Every deceased hope must be resurrected through and by our faith. It may look like the final countdown, but know you are not out for the count.

We are not ignorant of suffering; we must all go through hard times like Christ. God never promised that our journey would be met with a bed of ease. Nor did he say that being a follower of Christ would be effortless. Every believer will be met with challenges. Even in these agonizing times, we must hold fast to our faith. We cannot succumb to defeat. You are not defeated because greater lives inside you than he who lives inside the world. We must continue to face each obstacle by understanding we have victory on the other side.

Overcomers Understand There Are Opportunities in Obstacles

Too many Christians believe that trials and tribulations constantly happen because God does not care. On the contrary, he cares enough to strengthen us through our difficult times. With every obstacle comes a more incredible opportunity for God to be revealed. When God provides a block in our path, he does not mean for us to stumble over it clumsily. Instead, this is his opportunity to strengthen our belief, to make us stronger in him.

God does not bring obstacles in our lives for us to be defeated. Problems come in our lives so that he may be glorified through us. With each dilemma faced, God's power is revealed. God may not remove the block. But instead, he may cause the same problem to be the foundation of our victory.

Let's take a moment to consider Jacob's son, Joseph. At an early age, he experienced tremendous obstacles. For starters, his brothers hated him to death. Jacob's boys decided they weren't murderers but became the first human traffickers, selling their flesh and blood into slavery. From there, Joseph was given a nice cushy job, only to be wrongfully accused of rape by his boss's wife. Unfortunately for Joseph, the husband was the judge, jury, and executor and convicted him of this heinous sex crime. After being

I AM AN OVERCOMER.

handed a guilty verdict, he served seven years in Egypt's federal state pen.

For Joseph, there was no Innocence Project or Hebrew Lives Matter movement. However, there was an opportunity in his obstacle. Even though he was a prisoner, Joseph still held on to who he was in God. Joseph could have easily denied his father's teachings or spiritual gift but instead continued to let that be a part of him. Ironically, the same gift that seemed to be the root of his problems became his solution. Through his obstacle, Joseph seized the opportunity to free himself from prison. He used what God had given him to proclaim his innocence, instantly moving from prison to a presidential seat.

There is no obstacle too great for God, no problem too substantial for him to resolve. Troubles seemed to follow Joseph throughout his life, but in the end, God was glorified. We must understand that we will go through life trials and tribulations, yet there are opportunities in our obstacles. No matter our problem, we know everything works together for our good (Rom 8:28).

Overcomers Have Victory in Peace

It's pretty challenging to think that horrific problems like disease and death are here to profit us. It is human nature to become skeptical and question God when significant issues arise. Nevertheless, God will immerse us in peace during those most difficult times. Peace is a believer's gift from God. Unfortunately, this peace is not given to the world. It is exclusively reserved for God's elect. Even when faced with the most horrendous problems, God will cancel out our worries and engulf us in his peace.

On April 17, 2005, my world came to a screeching stop. We were on my sister's campus when I learned that my daughter's father was killed in Ramadi, Iraq. Instantly, the news hit me like a ton of bricks, and I remember collapsing to the ground in utter shock. It wasn't possible. He was just a small-town boy who was a star basketball player. *How could he possibly be gone? This can't be true. It's some dreadful mistake.* As a sea of strangers attempted to console my family, I thought of him, his family, and my now fatherless daughter.

I will trust you, God, I will trust you. This phrase was the mantra that I kept saying to myself repeatedly. I don't know why; it wasn't like I was that spiritual during that time. However, the phrase spilled out of my mouth, coming from the uttermost parts of my heart. I couldn't fathom why God would take my daughter's father. I couldn't comprehend it, but I knew I had to trust God.

Ironically, I had heard about the bombing on the news earlier that morning. I remember saying a quick prayer for the soldier's families as I watched. My simple request was to help their families and comfort them through this ordeal. Unbeknownst to me, I was praying for myself and am grateful I did.

Taking on so much responsibility for a twenty-five-year-old seemed too much to handle. There was no time to process his death in those moments as Veteran Affairs visited me, insurance agents, casualty assistant officer this, and sergeant that. I was overwhelmed and just wanted to take a moment to think about my daughter's future. Think about how we would carry on and survive without him in our world. I may have wondered, but I never worried.

Certainly, the Army takes care of its own, but God ultimately cared for me. I never worried about my daughter's emotional well-being, how we would survive financially, or how she would go on without her father in her life. Through it all, God provided for our every need. My daughter was taken care of financially, graduated college sixteen years later, and has loving grandparents who continue his memory. Again, I may have wondered, but I never worried. I never worried because I had the peace of God.

Peace is an overcomer's spiritual weapon. Satanic powers cannot stand as God's peace demolishes our adversary's battle plans (Rom 16:20). Our victory is in our peace. The world is plagued by the things they hear and see, yet as overcomers, we stand firm in the voice of Truth. Reacting in God's peace confuses Satan. The battleground is within our minds, and if our enemy can place seeds of worry, those seeds will grow into doubt and bloom into disbelief in God's Word. Yet, fighting life's battles with peace produces victory every time. We may often wonder about our problems, but we shouldn't worry.

Overcomers Stand Firm on God's Word

From Genesis to Revelation, the Bible is filled with scriptures of victory. We hear stories of biblical characters being victorious, which seems unreal. Unfortunately, we listen to them so much that we become immune to the reality that these things occurred as if they were fairytales. A young boy *did* defeat a giant, a man *did* depart a river, and a woman *did* save a nation. These stories are not fictional but are factual accounts of triumph. Those called to be overcomers use these tales of conquest as a foundation for their victory. Not only this, they recall the multiple times God showed himself strong in their lives.

God's word is a sword in battle. The wiles of Satan constantly attempt to knock us off the solid foundation of God's word. However, as Paul stated, we must stand. As believers, we must stand firmly in every promise God has written in the book. He has promised to save, heal, and deliver his people. Overcomers use scriptures as a weapon against Satan's battle plans. When our enemy shuts a door, God just won't reopen it, but he will demolish the foundation. God's word is powerful, active, and alive. We must learn how to operate every word as our weapon.

IT'S TIME TO SHARPEN YOUR BLADE

When Paul told believers to put on the whole armor of God, each piece was a defensive mechanism except for the sword of the spirit. The sword was the only offensive weapon mentioned as we fight with the Word of God. Satan attempts to use every lie to hinder us, yet we must combat it with God's Word. We must sharpen our swords. There is no use fighting in this battle with a dull blade. God's word is a powerful weapon, ready to be used as a double-edged sword, cutting both ways (Eph 6:17). We can use the sword of the Spirit on our enemies or the enemy within us, ourselves. Either way, we must understand the powerful weapon we hold in God's Word.

During the pandemic, my pastor admonished the church to pray scriptures. I pondered what she meant by this and started searching God's Word. Through studying, I realized that the Bible is a blueprint to victory. It is a mighty weapon for whatever obstacle we face. So to prevent Covid-19, I stood firm on Psalms 91:10, *"There shall no evil befall thee, neither shall any plague come nigh thy dwelling."* When everyone else around me was getting sick, this was my prayer. I used my weapon, and my household was protected.

Overcomers understand that the Word of God is a strong foundation on which his people can stand. We have victory and promises in God's Word. If we are in the midst of our battle, we can declare, "No weapon formed against me shall prosper" (Isa 54:17). Perhaps, we need financial help; we can say, "And my God will supply every need of ours according to his riches in glory in Christ Jesus" (Phil 4:19). Or even if we are sick, we can fight with, "But he *was* wounded for our transgressions, *he was* bruised for our iniquities: the chastisement of our peace *was* upon him; and with his stripes, we are healed" (Isa 53:5). Our weapon is the Word of God. We don't overcome this by standing on politicians' empty promises or scientific propaganda. However, we stand firm on the eternal Words of God.

Overcomers Activates Faith, Deactivates Facts

God's Words are a solid foundation that counteracts facts and activates our faith. There is nothing impossible for God. Facts are debunked when God is in control. When faced with awful news, overcomers don't worry about the details but place their faith in God. Putting our faith in God makes things that were once seen as factual now false.

I AM AN OVERCOMER.

God has a way of altering the course of natural truths. Recently, my community was shaken by a fatal car accident killing one of my former students. One of her sisters was in the hospital, fighting for her life. Every time the news came, it seemed she wouldn't make it. However, we began to pray against the scientific facts to ensure that faith discredits truth. The young lady died, and to say the least, I was puzzled.

My continued prayer was that she lived. So, when I got the news that she passed, I began to retreat to when my grandmother died. I remembered how earnestly I prayed for her; she died, and so did this young girl. Yet, both *did* live.

God allowed them to live past their circumstances so their families could say goodbye. My grandmother's eight children were with her when she departed this life. For the young girl, her mother and younger sister could still not see her until they were released. She continued to fight and live until she could see her family. The same day she died. The doctors thought she would have passed the same day of her accident, but she lived several days afterward. Despite her being pronounced brain dead, I believe that God knew her heart and allowed her to live despite her condition.

Overcomers activate faith during life's heartaches. Even when the outcome is not what we expected or thought, God's way is always perfect. As an overcomer, we believe in God over facts. He is the same God who healed the blind man, caused a person with paralysis to walk, and raised a young girl from the dead. He did those things then, so surely he can do them now. Facts say one thing, but God has the final word over them all.

Our confidence is not in our abilities but God's. He has given us the power of overcomers to walk triumphantly. We are more than conquerors; we are the glory of God, his victorious children. Trials and tribulations will happen, but they cannot destroy our overcomer's status. God merely requires that we walk uprightly, placing our trust in him. Once we can stand firm on his Word, we can defeat every obstacle. Therefore, there is no obstacle that you cannot conquer. No challenge is too enormous for you to solve, and no mountain is too high to scale. In fact, as an overcomer, you don't even have to climb the mountain. You can merely speak to it. That's the power granted to you as an overcomer. You can overcome any obstacle as God has given you the ability not only to overcome life's challenges but to overcome the world.

Chapter 10

I am predestined.

> And those he predestined, he also called; those he called, he also justified; those he justified, he also glorified.
>
> —ROMANS 8:30

OVER A DECADE AGO, I heard the voice of God saying, "They are waiting on you." They, being the youth of my church. After the brief moment of excitement had dwindled, my response was, "let them wait." Needless to say, I was not very enthusiastic about being called by God. I wanted to do my own thing, wear what I wanted, talk as I pleased, and surround myself with God's enemy, or as we call them, the world.

Nope, I was comfortably fine doing me every day until I felt like I was in a holding pattern. I was stuck in the same situation, the same obstacle, unable to move forward. Life seemed to pass me by until I questioned how long I would be stagnate in this position. It wasn't until I surrendered my will to God that I understood that my life wasn't mine.

If someone had told me years ago that I would be a minister, I would've put my drink down and laughed in their face. Looking back on those years, it would have been a far-fetched notion that God would choose a woman like myself. Even now, I'm in disbelief. God could have selected anyone out of the billion but took a chance on me. I believe God wanted a hot mess of a person to preach to other hot messes. However, God would say I was preselected for his perfect will, and so are you.

PREDESTINED, CALLED, JUSTIFIED, AND GLORIFIED

Those He Predestined

To understand predestination, let's unpack Romans 8:29–30. These verses have been particularly controversial as they open a can of worms to question if humans have free will or whether God's sovereign will is unilateral. I am going to argue that it is both. God has allowed all creation the ability to make decisions. However, on the flip side, God is omniscient, meaning he is all-knowing and appears to have preordained particular people to do his bidding.

Most Christians know Jeremiah 1:4–5, as it proclaims that God knew him before he was formed in the womb. The Lord had consecrated Jeremiah and appointed him a prophet over the nations before he was even born. When God spoke these words to him, Jeremiah was argumentatively young. Some even believe that he was as young as seventeen. Surely, as a teenager, he wasn't thinking about being a servant of God. More likely, his thoughts were like most teenage boys on the opposite sex and marriage during that time. However, God had other plans for Jeremiah that he did not know himself. No wonder he wept.

In Galatians 1:15, Paul also confirmed that God knew him before he was born. Here is another person God set apart for his divine will. We all know that Paul was a prosecutor of Christ before his transformation. God knew that Paul would have a sordid history, yet he still chose him to preach to the Jews and the Gentiles, becoming the most influential preacher of all time. Now here is the mind-boggling question. Since God appointed them before they were born, could they decline their appointment? Better yet, did God override their free will?

I AM PREDESTINED.

Truthfully, we have no idea. Chalk it up to another mystery of God's. However, I will state my two cents for what it is worth. I believe that God calls all of Creation to repentance, yet some people are just marked. Believers of Calvinism would perhaps disagree as they believe that God predetermines who will be saved[1].

On the contrary, I am sure that supporters of Arminianism would argue that humans have free will to choose or deny God[2]. However, I believe it's a mixture of the two theologies; call it Ruffianism. All people are given a free choice, yet God preselects specific individuals for a particular task.

When God formed Adam and Eve, I believe he did it with the expectation that they would not sin against him. Ironically, I like to think of it as a social experiment. I can almost see the pilot commercial. *What will happen when two perfect strangers are placed in Paradise, given everything they need and want? The only catch is they cannot eat from one tree. Stay tuned to determine if Adam and Eve will fall into "Temptation."* That's a reality show I would watch. Unfortunately, we already know the end. Despite God's goodness and provisions, Adam and Eve's free will ultimately led to disobedience, bringing sin into the world.

If God already knew sin would occur, why would he give us free will? Many people have pondered this question. Yet, the answer is that God loved us enough to create us solely in his divine image. No one controls God, and he has granted us the same free course to make our own decisions. Surely, he could have created submissive creatures to do what he wanted. However, God gave every human a mind to choose or reject him. It is ultimately our choice.

He Also Called

Therefore, all creation has been granted free will, yet I believe that God also preordains specific individuals for specific times.

1. Cynar, "Calvinism vs. Arminianism: What's The Difference?", lines 1 – 3.
2. Cynar, "Calvinism vs. Arminianism: What's The Difference?", lines 4 – 6.

Ephesians 4:11 declares that God appoints certain people within the fivefold ministry. These individuals are a part of the chosen called. Remember, all believers are called to do God's will, yet some are called upon for specific tasks that lead others further to Christ (2 Tim 1:9). The bible is filled with biblical characters God predestinated and called for a particular mission. However, since God predestinated some individuals, could they have escaped their calling?

I don't know how Paul felt when he was knocked off his beast; however, he didn't have much choice in his transformation if he felt like me. It's an inner torment. For years, I have heard stories from preachers who God called. Many describe an internal tugging, a feeling of urgency that persistently gnaws at them. Some have explained it as the unction of the Holy Ghost, while I described it like a pesky mosquito that wouldn't die, no matter how hard I swapped it. God's calling feels different for many people; however, for those who God truly calls, it appears that our inner man is unrestful until we surrender our will and accept the calling.

Surrendering our will is the first part of predestination. For years, I knew that God had called me to be a minister of the gospel. However, I fought hard against it, yet I couldn't outbox God. I tried. Every time I felt my heartstrings tug, I would increase every sin I was willing to do. I figured God would move on to the next willing participant if I sinned enough. He didn't. For some reason, he still came after me. His pursuit of me was pretty perplexing.

There is nothing special about me. I'm so unworthy, yet the Creator of this world chose me. Thinking more about it, I became more rebellious. I literally played Russian Roulette with my spiritual life because I did not want to surrender my will to God. However, it seemed that I had free will only to a certain degree.

Despite my spiritual battle with God, I ultimately chose him because I was preordained. I know that's an oxymoron, but it was a simple choice between life or death. I honestly felt my natural and spiritual life would be endangered if I did not accept God's calling. Especially when God asked, "how much longer are you going to make me wait?" That one question terrified me into submission. Time was running out, and I knew I better choose God.

The fact is that when God calls us, there is no ignoring the Caller Id. God will keep calling until we decide to answer. I am infamously famous for not answering my phone. I screen every call; ironically, I did the same in the spirit. Yet, God's call became more urgent for me. I started to wonder what would happen if God stopped calling. Would that be my last chance to answer?

I knew God hand's were upon me, but I didn't want him to use me the way he intended. I was fine playing a background role in the church, just as a supporting cast member. No way did I want to be a lead performer behind a pulpit. I wasn't ready to give up my life as Jesus gave his for mine.

Thinking on it now, it was selfish. Yet, I felt it was not the most desirable thing to be chosen by God, mainly because nothing was alluring about me. I was a sinner. A disgusting sinner that did awful things, and there was no way that anyone would believe that God chose the likes of me.

Those He Called, He Also Justified

I was so undeserving of God's love, so deep in sin, that God's grace utterly did not seem that sufficient. Even if I could accept that God still loved and forgave me, there was no way he would call upon me to do his will. I was a willful sinner, a willing participant for our adversary. I was hypocritical and did not care. I told God that I liked the sins that I was committing. Imagine that. I was bold enough to confess to the Almighty God that I liked what he hated.

Thankfully, God delivered me from a life of sin, yet I still did not feel worthy enough to be used for his glory. Ironically, God seems to call some ruthless and unworthy characters for his great purposes. I was neither a prostitute like Rahab nor a drunk like Noah. I wasn't a murderer like Moses or a con artist like Zacchaeus. However, I still did not feel like I had any redeeming qualities. There was no way I could preach to a congregation that had witnessed my youthful rebellion firsthand. How could I teach God's word to people who taught it to me, and I willingly rejected it? Yet, when God calls, he has a plan for justification.

Despite drowning in low self-worth, I accepted the call into the ministry. I still feel unfit, yet, I am stronger because God proves himself every time I preach. This is not boasting but merely justification into action. Those God calls for a desired purpose; he will also justify. I am sure that people wondered why God called me into the ministry. I was openly rebellious, yet God transformed my rebellion into submission, just like he changed Peter's pride to humility and Jacob's deception to honesty. God changed and justified me through his grace and mercy.

I remember questioning God why he preordained and called me into the ministry. His simple answer was that my heart was towards him. Justification merely means God undoes and replaces our unredeemable qualities with more desirable usable ones. Ironically, God alters our behaviors from what once were to the very opposite. I went from defiance to reliance. David went from uncontrollable lust to self-discipline, and Moses went from aggression to humbleness.

It is remarkable to think how God molds and transforms our lives for his divine purposes. God will remove the stain of sin despite our past, altering our lives. Not only do we become the righteousness of God, but he also justifies us. God will explain it without explanation. God proves us through and by his righteousness. Once we accept him, he uses what we once were to show the glory manifested in us through faith.

Those He Justified, He Also Glorified

God glorifies those he has justified and called. I know this is a mind-boggling concept that God will glorify us, but it is written in black and white, Romans 8:30. It's God's process coming full circle. First, he predestinates our lives for a specific assignment. He then calls upon us to do the task; once we accept, the Lord will justify his plan in our lives, and then out of our obedience, he will glorify us. Mind-boggling, right? How is it that we went from filth to glory, that a God worthy of glorification returns it to his children?

We often talk about glorifying God; however, let's examine what it means when God said he would bless those he has preordained and called. First, when we accept our God-given purpose, God will sanctify us, meaning he sets us apart. God setting us apart signifies God's love and our importance to him.

Think about it like our glassware. Most people don't mix their crystal goblets with paper or plastic cups. Instead, they separate them despite the objects having the same function. No one cares if a plastic cup gets misplaced. However, crystal glass is of value and worth. God separates us because there is worth in our vessel that is precious and costly.

Ironically, we were the cheap plastic, yet God changed us into something we were not. Our sins should have discounted us into every being considered for God's purpose. Yet, God took the filth of our iniquities, transforming us from rags to riches. There is no way a paper cup can alter its appearance to resemble a crystal in the natural. However, God changes us from a vessel of dishonor to honor. Then as it is written in 2 Timothy 2:21, God will set us apart for particular purposes and good works despite our past deeds.

Our past was dishonorable, yet God makes us worthy, promoting and elevating us within our purpose. This is why we must understand the benefits of saying yes to God. When we give God our yes, he will, in turn, say yes to us. God's yes in our lives is loaded with spiritual and natural benefits as he is not slack in his promises. Our full, wholehearted acceptance of our God-given purpose will bring forth continued provisional blessings in our lives.

An Invitation to Predestination

The parable of the wedding feast provides symbolism for our predestination (Matt 22: 1 – 14). In the parable, a king sent invitations to his son's wedding. However, those invited did not want to attend. So the king extended his hospitality to everyone to come to the feast. Obviously, the king was God who extended the invitation to the Jews for salvation, but they rejected Christ. Therefore, the offer was sent to everyone.

God has invited us all to salvation through his Son, Jesus Christ. In his divine wisdom, the Lord knew that his Creation would falter to sin, so he preordained that his Son would be the slain lamb that would take our place. Even though many have accepted the invitation to salvation, a few are still restricted.

We found out that one guest was ill-attired and escorted out of the banquet. I found this quite puzzling as I wondered what was wrong with his clothing. Did his sandals not match his robe? Perhaps the invitation required everyone to wear purple, and he showed up in black. Maybe he was too poor to spend his last goat on a cloak. Surely, our loving God wouldn't turn anyone away because they wore Walmart instead of Armani or Valentino, would he? I would, but not God. No matter the reason, the guest was kicked out of the wedding due to his poor fashion choice. How embarrassing, whatever happened to come as you are?

Well, we are missing a critical piece to the puzzle. During biblical times, many affluent families provided wedding garments for their guests. Therefore, the king undoubtedly supplied his invitees with beautiful attire, yet there was that one person who decided they wanted to wear their own clothing. There is always that one defiant person who goes against the demands of the invitation because they want to be unique. Unfortunately, their individuality came at a high cost as the king bound him, sending the guest into utter darkness where there was weeping and gnashing of teeth (Matt 22:13).

That was pretty harsh. One lousy fashion faux pas, and to hell they went. However, it wasn't what they wore; it was more like what they were unwilling to give up. The guest was invited to the wedding of the century and was reluctant to depart with their rags. I don't care if it was Queen Sheba's designer; their outfit was considered rags compared to what the king had in store. Rejecting to wear God's garments of love, peace, and salvation means we wear rebellion accessorized by doubt.

I AM PREDESTINED.

To be truthful, I'm searching my heart because even as a minister, I feel like I am trying to wear God's fashion with mistrust stilettos. So, trust me when I say that I know that it is hard to accept predestination. I get it because I feel like I am being pushed into being something that I am not. I'm not ready to move forward in God when I am barely comfortable with my title as a minister. I know God has predestined me, but do I have to move so fast in my predestination? The terrifying truth is that if God requires me to move fast, there is nothing I can do about it.

Everyone has been selected for a specific task, although some reject the invitation while others accept it. Yet like the ill-dressed guest, some will accept the invitation but not the requirements. Unfortunately, they want salvation and all the benefits of Calvary but cannot handle the constraints of surrendering their will to God.

God has predestined all of us for an excellent task with greater rewards, but we must be willing to accept the invitation and the conditions. We can't fully accept the invitation of predestination if we show up in our outdated will, yet we must wear the glorious plan of God for our lives.

That may be easier said than done as I think about Judas, poor Judas. Poor preselected Judas will be forever remembered as the sell-out thief who orchestrated the murder of our precious Lord and Savior, Jesus Christ. Was he truly preselected to be the disciple that would ultimately become one of the most hated men of the Bible? However, as I frequently say, someone had to do it. Someone had to betray Jesus because if it were not for Judas, then we would be lost.

I always wondered if there could have been an alternate ending. For example, what if Jesus turned himself into the Romans? Could Judas's earthly task be unassigned, leading to him being remembered as a good, faithful disciple? Alas, that is not the case, and somebody had to betray Jesus and Judas picked the shortest straw. The fact is that God's plan is sovereign, and he will use those he desires to fulfill his divine plan. Now, I am more thankful that God called me to be a minister than a betrayer.

The reality is that no one truly knows why Judas betrayed Jesus. However, we do know that scripture had to be fulfilled. Hundreds of years prior, David prophesied Judas's deceit (Ps 41:9). Meaning that someone was going to betray Jesus. We know that Satan entered Judas during the last supper to fulfill that prophecy (Luke 22:3). Jesus ultimately knew that Judas would be the one that would betray him. Maybe that's why Jesus selected the untrustworthy outsider to be a part of the twelve. Again, no one knows, but one thing that cannot be argued is that his betrayal was predestinated.

God has given each person free will to elect him as Lord. Even though the invitation has been extended, the unfortunate truth is that many people outright choose to live ungodlily. However, it does not mean that God's predestination is invalid. As I stated before, I don't think God intended anyone to be sent to eternal damnation. I earnestly believe that God desires salvation for all people. He had a plan to extend the invitation to the tree of life, yet many instead choose to live for eternal death.

As God's Creation, we have the right to choose our pathway. Continuing with my Ruffinism theology, I believe God is sovereign, knowing all, but allows freedom of choice within our predestination. God does not preselect those who will inherit the Kingdom of Heaven nor more than he damns individuals to the fiery pit.

Instead, I believe our two ways are predestined. There are two roads, the Strait and the Broad (Matthew 7:13–14). I imagine God has prepared our life journey, placing detours and traffic jams on our route. We can stay on the "straight and narrow" path that leads to Christ, trusting him through the roadblocks. Or we can travel a more open road, depending on our own life's map leading us to destruction. I think we have two alternate endings, Heaven or Hell. God has predestined both of our endings as he is sovereign, yet we choose the path we take.

I AM PREDESTINED.

Which path will you choose?

At times our life's trajectory is out of sync with our predestination. However, whatever was for us, against us, or done to us was all in God's plan. The plan of God is like a GPS. God knows our final destination; however, we get off track. Like in the natural, we tend to follow our instincts without relying on the GPS. We often learn that it is better to listen to Siri than our thoughts.

Once I was traveling, my GPS took me off the interstate into unfamiliar territories. Despite wanting to stay on the usual road, I followed the British-speaking voice towards the unbeaten path. It wasn't that bad at first until I found myself in the backwoods of some hick town, terrified my GPS was leading me straight to a Klan meeting. I took that moment to increase my prayer life, worrying that I would never see the interstate again.

Then I saw it. The most beautiful faded blue sign that was leading back to I-95. I followed the arrows leading back to civilization without hesitation despite my GPS begging for a U-Turn. I was almost there. I could see lights, buildings, and cars. Beautiful unmovable, stagnated cars. Vehicles that hadn't moved for an hour. Unfortunately, I ignored Alexa as she only attempted to decrease my hardship, yet I was too afraid of my surroundings and didn't trust the plan.

God attempts to order our steps, but we decide to take another route because we ultimately don't trust his plan. We frequently get off course, making U-turns missing the mark, skipping the straight and narrow road God intended for us. Then there are traffic jams, and we feel like we are not moving fast enough. Instead of waiting, we decided to find another way to rush our arrival when God wanted us to stand still, knowing that the waiting would prevent unseen dangers. Yet, we choose to take control because the promised destination seems out of reach. Thankfully, no matter how many detours we take, God still allows us to arrive at our promised land.

Just like the Israelites, each believer has their own promised lands. It might not be flowing with milk or honey, but it is destined for you. God has provided several promises to his children within the bible. However, God also has preordained specific blessings as well. Perhaps it is a business venture, a dream home, getting married, or graduating from college. God is not slack or slow in his promises. Unfortunately, like the Israelites, we are too busy wandering in the wilderness.

The Israelites roamed the wilderness for forty years when it should have only been a couple of weeks, maybe less than ten days. God had promised them Canaan, yet their lack of faith gave them an extended stay in the all-inclusive resort of Kadesh-Barnea. Milk and honey were abundant in Canaan, yet they enjoyed fresh manna and quails for breakfast, lunch, and dinner. Well, at least no one had to ask, "What's for dinner?" for thirty-eight years.

Here is the reality. Despite the Israelites being in the wilderness, God still provided. Instead of seeking after God's promises, they lived comfortably in God's provisions. We are Father Abraham's seed because we continuously live contentedly in God's conditions when he says, "I have more for you."

Aren't you tired of eating manna and quail? God has milk and honey, promised blessings in store for you. God has predestinated natural and spiritual benefits for our lives, yet we continuously wander in our faithless wilderness.

Our predestined blessings and promises are waiting to be fulfilled. God had established the Israelites' path, and he is the same God who designed our course. He knows the roadblocks faced and the detours that need to be taken. God has created a specific journey for each one of our lives. Isn't it about time that we recognize the plan of God, travel it, stepping out on faith?

Life challenges often derail our faith. Nevertheless, we have to continue to move forward. We cannot afford to be stagnated in the wilderness. I know that we tend to wonder about the course of our lives and the direction God is taking us. If we can be honest, it is a bit intimidating. Yet, we have the best guide who will remove hindrances from our path to continue our journey. Perhaps the obstacle is sickness, financial, spiritual, or familial. Regardless of our hurdles, God sees them and designed the pebbles in our road to increase our faith.

This journey is not for the faint at heart. It requires steadfastness and trusting the plan of God. The mere fact is that once we decide to travel God's path, we will be met with foreseeable barriers. We know obstacles will arise, but we must understand that God is greater. Each heartache and disappointment will be the stepping stone to strengthen us on our journey.

There is a reason why James said to count it all joy when we face various trials. It is only testing our faith to produce unwavering patience. However, James goes a step further, saying, "but let patience have its perfect work, that you may be perfect and complete, lacking nothing" (Jas 1: 2–4). That is worth repeating. If we travel the path God intended for our lives, we will lack absolutely nothing.

Trials and tribulations will be a part of our journey. We were predestinated to go through certain heartaches, which may not be easy to understand. No one escapes life without suffering as our Lord and Savior experienced grief. Yet, I believe it's better to suffer with God than travel an easy road with Satan. Our suffering brings forth more incredible blessings on our journey. Each trial makes us that much stronger, and we must continue to travel the path God has established for our lives. Our problems cannot hinder the move of God. God has predestined our course, and we cannot afford to become idled on the path.

Our path is solely ours and ours alone. Jeremiah 29:11 (AMP) says, "For I know the plans *and* thoughts that I have for you,' says the Lord, 'plans for peace *and* well-being and not for disaster, to give you a future and a hope." God is always in control of our lives, with preordained blessings. However, are we truly on course for every benefit, or will we get to our destination and find boxes labeled "missed opportunities" because we are too afraid of our destiny?

If I can be blatantly honest, I am afraid at times. People have spoken so many things in my life that my course seems intimidating. However, for sure, I am learning to trust God. I understand that God has equipped me with every supply I need for my journey. Gratefully, he has done the same for you. We must know that we will have obstacles along the way, but each challenge brings us closer to our final destination. God will not leave or forsake us during our travel. He wants us to prosper and reach his plan for our lives. We need to decide if we will trust God or if we will derail.

The choice is ours; which path will you choose?

Bibliography

Cynar, Mike. "Calvinism vs. Arminianism: What's The Difference?" https://jesuswithoutreligion.com/calvinism-vs-arminianism/
Fairchild, Mary. "How Did God Appear to Man in the Old Testament?" https://www.learnreligions.com/what-is-theophany-4064725
McMenamin, Cindi. "What Does Reverence Mean, and How to Practice Daily Reverence?" https://www.crosswalk.com/faith/spiritual-life/what-does-reverence-mean.html